THE
DISUNITING
OF
AMERICA

BOOKS
BY
ARTHUR M.
SCHLESINGER JR.

ORESTES A. BROWNSON

THE AGE OF JACKSON

THE VITAL CENTER

THE GENERAL AND THE PRESIDENT
(WITH RICHARD ROVERE)

THE CRISIS OF THE OLD ORDER

THE COMING OF THE NEW DEAL

THE POLITICS OF UPHEAVAL

A THOUSAND DAYS: JOHN F. KENNEDY
IN THE WHITE HOUSE

THE BITTER HERITAGE

THE CRISIS OF CONFIDENCE

THE IMPERIAL PRESIDENCY

ROBERT KENNEDY AND HIS TIMES

THE CYCLES OF AMERICAN HISTORY

ARTHUR M. SCHLESINGER JR.

WHITTLE DIRECT BOOKS

The Larger Agenda Series is a registered trademark of Whittle Communications L.P.

Photography: Gunnar Myrdal, The Bettmann Archive, page 8; Israel Zangwill, Library of Congress, page 11; Horace Kallen, courtesy of Harvard University Archives, page 13; William Thompson, F.P.G. International, page 25; John V. Kelleher, courtesy of Harvard University Archives, page 26; Maulana Karenga, courtesy of California State University Long Beach, page 30; Asa Hilliard, Ellsworth Davis/*The Washington Post*, page 31; Leonard Jeffries, courtesy of City College of New York, page 34; John Henrik Clarke, courtesy of Clarke, page 36; Arthur Schlesinger Jr. and father, Burt Glinn/Magnum Photos, page 42; W.E.B. Du Bois, Library of Congress, page 45; William Raspberry, courtesy of Raspberry, page 47; Frederick Douglass, Library of Congress, page 51; John Hope Franklin, courtesy of Franklin, page 53; Diane Ravitch, G. Paul Burnett/*The New York Times*, page 54; August Wilson, Geof Kern, page 60; Richard Rodriguez, Roger Ressmeyer, page 62; Dinesh D'Souza, Susan Muniak/courtesy of Free Press, page 65; Tiananmen Square, Peter Charlesworth/JB Pictures, page 77.

Illustrations: J. Hector St. John de Crèvecoeur, Library of Congress, page 2; emblem of the Order of United Americans, Culver Pictures Inc., page 9; *Puck* cartoon, The Larger Agenda Collection, page 10.

Library of Congress Catalog Card Number: 91-65510
Schlesinger, Arthur M., Jr.
The Disuniting of America
ISBN 1-879736-00-4
ISSN 1046-364X

The Larger Agenda Series ®

The Larger Agenda Series presents original short books by distinguished authors on subjects of importance to managers and policymakers in business and the public sector.

The series is edited and published by Whittle Books, a business unit of Whittle Communications L.P. A new book appears approximately every other month. The series reflects a broad spectrum of responsible opinions. In each book the opinions expressed are those of the author, not the publisher or the advertiser.

I welcome your comments on this unique endeavor.

William S. Rukeyser
Editor in Chief

CONTENTS

FOREWORD

"What then is the American, this new man?" This was the question famously asked two centuries ago by a Frenchman who called himself J. Hector St. John de Crèvecoeur. Crèvecoeur had emigrated to the American colonies in 1759 at the age of 24. In time he married an American woman and settled on a farm in Orange County, New York. An astute observer of American ways, he posed his celebrated question in *Letters From an American Farmer*, a book published in London during the American Revolution. Translated into French, German, and Dutch, Crèvecoeur's *Letters* became a European bestseller.

What led Europeans to read Crèvecoeur? What led so many to follow his example and cross a dangerous ocean to a new world? In this "great American asylum," Crèvecoeur wrote, the poor of Europe, leaving sore affliction and pinching penury behind, are seeking a new life—and finding it. "Every thing has tended to regenerate them; new laws, a new mode of living, a new social system; here they are become men: in Europe they were as so many useless plants . . . mowed down by want, hunger, and war. . . ."

Crèvecoeur ruminated over the astonishing diversity of the settlers—"a mixture of English, Scotch, Irish, French, Dutch, Germans, and Swedes," a "strange mixture of blood" that you could find in no other country. He recalled a family whose grandfather was English, whose wife was Dutch, whose son married a Frenchwoman, and whose present four sons had married women of different nationalities. "From this promiscuous breed," he wrote, "that race now called Americans have arisen."

The word *race* as used in the 18th and 19th centuries generally meant what we mean by nationality today; thus people spoke of "the English race," "the German race," and so on. What, Crèvecoeur mused, were the characteristics of this suddenly emergent American race? "What then was the American, this new man?" (Twentieth-century readers must overlook 18th-century male obliviousness to the existence of women.) He provided a classic answer to his own question: "*He* is an American, who leaving behind him all his ancient prejudices and manners, receives new ones from the new mode of life he has embraced, the new government he obeys, and the new rank he holds. The American is a new man, who acts upon new principles. . . . *Here individuals of all nations are melted into a new race of men."*

Crèvecoeur's conception was of a brand-new nationality created by individuals who, in repudiating their homelands and joining to make new lives, melted away ancient ethnic differences. Most of those intrepid Europeans who had torn up their roots to brave the wild Atlantic and attain America wanted to forget a horrid past and to embrace a hopeful future. They *expected* to become Americans. Their goals were escape, deliverance, assimilation. They saw America as a transforming nation, banishing old loyalties and forging a new national identity based on common political ideals.

This conception prevailed through most of the two centuries of the history of the United States. But lately a new conception has arisen. In a nation marked by an even stranger mixture of blood, Crèvecoeur's question is asked once more, with new intensity and new answers. Today many Americans turn away from the historic goal of "a new race of man." The escape from origins has given way to the search for roots. The "ancient prejudices and manners" disclaimed by Crèvecoeur have made a surprising comeback.

This 1786 portrait of J. Hector St. John de Crèvecoeur was published on the frontispiece of his popular book *Letters From an American Farmer*.

The new gospel condemns Crèvecoeur's vision of individuals of all nations melted into a new race in favor of an opposite vision: a nation of groups, differentiated in their ancestries, inviolable in their diverse identities. The contemporary ideal is shifting from assimilation to ethnicity, from integration to separatism.

The ethnic upsurge has had some healthy consequences. The republic has at last begun to give long-overdue recognition to the role and achievements of groups subordinated and ignored during the high noon of male Anglo-Saxon dominance—women, Americans of South and East European ancestry, black Americans, Indians, Hispanics, Asians. There is far better understanding today of the indispensable contributions minorities have made to American civilization.

But the cult of ethnicity, pressed too far, exacts costs. It may even portend a new turn in American life. Instead of a transformative nation with an identity all its own, America increasingly sees itself as preservative of old identities. Instead of a nation composed of individuals making their own free choices, America increasingly sees itself as composed of groups more or less indelible in their ethnic character. The national ideal had once been *e pluribus unum*. Are we now to belittle *unum* and glorify *pluribus*? Will the center hold? or will the melting pot yield to the Tower of Babel?

A struggle to redefine the national identity is taking place. It is taking place in many arenas—in our politics, our voluntary organizations, our churches, our language—and in no arena more crucial than our system of education. The schools and colleges of the republic train the citizens of the future. They have always been battlegrounds for debates over beliefs, philosophies, values. Today our educational institutions face intense pressure to revise academic curricula to meet the needs—and the demands—of an increasingly pluralistic society.

What students learn in schools vitally affects other arenas of American life—the way we see and treat other Americans, the way we conceive the purpose of the republic. The debate about the curriculum is a debate about what it means to be an American. What is ultimately at stake is the shape of the American future.

"Try telling your kid you fly a warehouse for a living."

Mark McNair
Pilot, Indianapolis

By using Federal Express planes to deliver everything from computer parts to airline tickets just when they're needed, companies are discovering that they can keep inventory costs from soaring.

CHAPTER
1

"A NEW RACE"?

At the beginning America was seen as a severing of roots, a liberation from the stifling past, an entry into a new life, an interweaving of separate ethnic strands into a new national design. "We have it in our power," said Thomas Paine for the revolutionary generation, "to begin the world all over again." The unstated national motto was "Never look back." "The Past is dead, and has no resurrection," wrote Herman Melville. " . . . The Past is the text-book of tyrants; the Future the Bible of the Free."

I

And the future was America—not so much a nation, Melville said, as a world. "You can not spill a drop of American blood without spilling the blood of the whole world. On this Western Hemisphere all tribes and people are forming into one federated whole. . . . " For Ralph Waldo Emerson too, like Crèvecoeur, like Melville, America was the distillation of the multifarious planet. As the burning of the temple at Corinth had melted and intermixed silver and gold to produce Corinthian brass, "a new compound more precious than any," so, Emerson wrote in his journal, in America, in this "asylum of all nations, the energy of Irish, Germans, Swedes, Poles, & Cossacks, & all the European tribes—of the Africans, & of the Polynesians, will construct a new race . . . as vigorous as the new Europe which came out of the smelting pot of the Dark Ages. . . . "

Melville was a novelist, Emerson an essayist; both were poets. But George Washington was a sternly practical man. Yet he believed no less ardently in the doctrine of the "new race." "The bosom of America," Washington said, "is open . . . to the oppressed and persecuted of all Nations and Religions." But immigrants who nestled as groups in the national bosom might retain the "Language, habits and principles (good or bad) which they bring with them." Let them therefore settle as individuals, prepared for "intermixture with our people." Then they would be "assimilated to our customs, measures and laws: in a word, soon become *one people*."

John Quincy Adams, another sternly practical man, similarly insisted on the exclusiveness of the new American identity. When a German baron contemplating emigration interviewed Adams as secretary of state, Adams admonished his visitor that emigrants had to make up their minds to one thing: "*They must cast off the European skin, never to resume it. They must look forward to their posterity rather than backward to their ancestors. . . .*"

But how could Crèvecoeur's "promiscuous breed" be transformed into a "new race"? How was Emerson's "smelting pot" to fuse such disparate elements into Washington's "one people"? This question pre-occupied another young Frenchman who arrived in America three quarters of a century after Crèvecoeur. "Imagine, my dear friend, if you can," Alexis de Tocqueville wrote back to France, "a society formed of all the nations of the world . . . people having different languages, beliefs, opinions: in a word, a society without roots, without memories, without prejudices, without routines, without common ideas, without a national character, yet a hundred times happier than our own." What alchemy could make this miscellany into a single society?

The answer, Tocqueville concluded, lay in the commitment of Americans to democracy and self-government. Civic participation, Tocqueville argued in *Democracy in America*, was the great educator and the great unifier.

> How does it happen that in the United States, where the inhabitants have only recently immigrated to the land which they now occupy, and brought neither customs nor traditions with them there; where they met one another for the first time with no previous acquaintance; where, in short, the instinctive love of country can scarcely exist; how does it happen that every one takes as zealous an interest in the affairs of his township, his country, and the whole state as if they were his own? It is because everyone, in his sphere, takes an active part in the government of society.

Immigrants, Tocqueville said, become Americans through the exercise of the political rights and civic responsibilities bestowed on them by the Declaration of Independence and the Constitution.

Half a century later, when the next great foreign commentator on American democracy, James Bryce, wrote *The American Commonwealth*, immigration had vastly increased and diversified. Bryce's European friends expected that it would take a very long time for America to assimilate these "heterogeneous elements." What struck Bryce, on the contrary, was what had struck Tocqueville: "the amazing solvent power which American institutions, habits, and ideas exercise upon newcomers of all races . . . quickly dissolving and assimilating the foreign bodies that are poured into her mass."

A century after Tocqueville, another foreign visitor, Gunnar Myrdal of Sweden, called the cluster of ideas, institutions, and habits "the American Creed." Americans "of all national origins, regions, creeds, and colors," Myrdal wrote in 1944, hold in common "the *most explicitly expressed* system of general ideals" of any country in the West: the ideals of the essential dignity and equality of all human beings, of inalienable rights to freedom, justice, and opportunity.

The schools teach the principles of the Creed, Myrdal said; the churches preach them; the courts hand down judgments in their terms. Myrdal saw the Creed as the bond that links all Americans, including nonwhite minorities, and as the spur forever goading Americans to live up to their principles. "America," Myrdal said, "is continuously struggling for its soul."

II

The late Gunnar Myrdal, a professor of economics at Stockholm, wrote the classic work on racism in America.

The American Creed had its antecedents, and these antecedents lay primarily in a British inheritance as recast by a century and a half of colonial experience. How really new then was the "new race"? Crèvecoeur's vision implied an equal blending of European stocks, and Emerson's smelting pot generously added Cossacks, Africans, and Polynesians. In fact, the majority of the population of the 13 colonies and the weight of its culture came from Great Britain.

Having cleared most of North America of their French, Spanish, and Dutch rivals, the British were free to set the mold. The language of the new nation, its laws, its institutions, its political ideas, its literature, its customs, its precepts, its prayers, primarily derived from Britain. Crèvecoeur himself wrote his book not in his native French but in his acquired English. The "curse of Babel," Melville said, had been revoked in America, "and the language they shall speak shall be the language of Britain."

The smelting pot thus had, unmistakably and inescapably, an Anglo-centric flavor. For better or worse, the white Anglo-Saxon Protestant tradition was for two centuries—and in crucial respects still is—the dominant influence on American culture and society. This tradition provided the standard to which other immigrant nationalities were expected to conform, the matrix into which they would be assimilated.

But as the 19th century proceeded, non-Anglo immigration gathered speed. European peasants who may never have dared go 20 miles from their birthplaces now undertook the unimaginable adventure of a journey across perilous seas to a strange land in search of a new life. The land was indeed strange; and they could not but feel a need for reassurance and security. So at first they tended to cling to their compatriots and to the language, schools, churches they brought with them. These ethnic enclaves served as staging areas for regrouping and basic training before entry was made into the larger and riskier American life.

These immigrants came principally from western and northern Europe. The Anglos often disliked the newcomers, disdained their uncouth presence, feared their alien religions and folkways. Germans and Scandinavians were regarded as clannish in their fidelity to the language and customs of the old country. The German fondness for beer gardens and jolly Sundays excited puritanical disapproval. The Irish were regarded as shiftless and drunken; moreover, they were papists, and their fealty to Rome, it was said, meant they could never become loyal Americans. They were subjected to severe discrimination in employment and were despised by genteel society. W.E.B. Du Bois, the black scholar, testified that when he grew up in Great Barrington, Massachusetts, in the 1870s, "the racial angle was more clearly defined against the Irish than against me."

As the flow of immigrants increased, so did resentment among the old-timers. By the 1850s immigrants made up half the population of New York and outnumbered native-born Americans in Chicago. Nativist organizations sprang up, like the Supreme Order of the Star-Spangled Banner and its political front, the American Party, calling for a lengthened naturalization process and curtailment of the political rights of the foreign-born. They were referred to as Know-Nothings because members of the Supreme Order, when asked about their secret oaths and rituals, would reply, "I know nothing."

The emblem of the Order of United Americans, a nativist group allied with the Know-Nothings, was published in an 1852 edition of The Republic.

In 1856 the Know-Nothings even ran a former president, Millard Fillmore, as their presidential candidate. "Our progress in degeneracy appears to me to be pretty rapid," observed Abraham Lincoln. "As a nation, we began by declaring that '*all men are created equal.*' We now practically read it 'all men are created equal, *except negroes.*' When the Know-Nothings get control, it will read 'all men are created equal, except negroes, *and foreigners, and catholics.*'"

But the Know-Nothing party fell as quickly as it rose. In the century and a half since, despite recurrent xenophobic outbursts, no nativist political party has appeared to take its place. However prejudiced white Anglo-Saxons were in practice, they were ashamed to endorse nativism in principle. Equally important, an expanding economy in an under-populated country required a steady influx of new hands. Immigration alleviated the labor shortage, and economic need overpowered moral and aesthetic repugnance.

The pre-Civil War immigrants steadily turned into Americans. "The frontier," in the words of its great historian, Frederick Jackson Turner, "promoted the formation of a composite nationality. . . . In the crucible of the frontier the immigrants were Americanized, liberated, and fused into a mixed race, English in neither nationality nor characteristics." In the crucible of the cities too assimilation proceeded apace. Even "the Irish immigrant's son," Bryce reported in 1888, "is an American citizen for all other purposes, even if he retain, which he seldom does, the hereditary Anglophobia."

III

After the Civil War came the so-called "new" immigration from southern and eastern Europe. Over 27 million arrived in the half-century from Lee's surrender at Appomattox to America's entry into the First World War—more than the total population of the country in 1850. The new immigrants—Italians, Poles, Hungarians, Czechs, Slovaks, Russians, Jews—settled mainly in the cities, where their bizarre customs, dress, languages, and religions excited new misgivings.

Yet the old faith in the power of Bryce's "amazing solvent" to fulfill Washington's conception of Americans as "one people" held fast. However much they suffered from social prejudice, the newcomers were not barred from civic participation, and civic participation indoctrinated them in the fundamentals of the American Creed. They altered the ethnic composition of the country, but they preserved the old ambition to become Americans.

The fastidious Henry James, revisiting his native land in 1904 after many years abroad, was at first dismayed by the alien bustle of Ellis Island. But he soon understood and appreciated "the ceaseless process of the recruiting of our race, of the plenishing of our huge national *pot-au-*

Joseph Keppler and Frederick Opper's early-20th-century cartoon portrayed German emigrants who were escaping oppression in their fatherland. It was published in Keppler's German-language *Puck*, a New York City weekly.

feu, of the introduction of fresh . . . foreign matter into our heterogeneous system." Though he wondered at times what immigration would do to Americans "ethnically, and thereby physiognomically, linguistically, *personally*," though he saw at times "the 'ethnic' apparition" sitting like a skeleton at the feast, he was more impressed by the "colossal" machinery that so efficiently converted the children of immigrants into Americans—the political and social habit, the common school, the newspaper, all so reliably producing what James called "the 'ethnic' synthesis." He spoke with something like awe about "the cauldron of the 'American' character."

New race, one people, smelting pot, *pot-au-feu*, cauldron—the original faith received its most celebrated metaphor a few years after James's visitation. In 1908 a play by Israel Zangwill, an English writer of Russian Jewish origin, opened in Washington. *The Melting-Pot* tells the story of a young Russian Jewish composer in New York. David Quixano's artistic ambition is to write a symphony expressing the vast, harmonious interweaving of races in America, and his personal hope is to overcome racial barriers and marry Vera, a beautiful Christian girl. "America," David cries, "is God's crucible, the great Melting-Pot where all the races of Europe are melting and re-forming! . . . Here you stand in your fifty groups, with your fifty languages . . . and your fifty blood hatreds. . . . A fig for your feuds and vendettas! Germans and Frenchmen, Irishmen and Englishmen, Jews and Russians—into the Crucible with you all! God is making the American."

Israel Zangwill, playwright of *The Melting-Pot*, was photographed by the celebrated J. E. Purdy of Boston in 1905.

The climactic scene takes place on the roof garden of a lower-Manhattan settlement house. In the background the Statue of Liberty gleams in the sunset. The composer, alone with Vera, gestures toward the city:

> There she lies, the great Melting-Pot—listen! Can't you hear the roaring and the bubbling? Ah, what a stirring and a seething! Celt and Latin, Slav and Teuton, Greek and Syrian,—black and yellow—
>
> VERA (*softly nestling to him*): Jew and Gentile—
>
> DAVID: Yes, East and West, and North and South, the palm and the pine, the pole and the equator, the crescent and the cross. . . . Here shall they all unite to build the Republic of Man and the Kingdom of God. Ah, Vera, what is the glory of Rome and Jerusalem where all nations and races come to worship and look back, compared with the glory of America, where all races and nations come to labour and look forward! . . . (*Far back, like a lonely, guiding star, twinkles over the darkening water the torch of the Statue of Liberty. From below comes up the softened sound of voices and instruments joining in 'My Country, 'tis of Thee.' The curtain falls slowly.*)

When the curtain fell in Washington and the author walked onstage, President Theodore Roosevelt called from his box: "That's a great play,

Mr. Zangwill, that's a great play." "I'm not a Bernard Shaw man or Ibsen man, Mrs. Zangwill," T. R. later told the playwright's wife. "No, *this* is the stuff." Zangwill subsequently dedicated the printed play to Roosevelt. *The Melting-Pot* played before rapt audiences across the country. Jane Addams of Hull-House in Chicago observed that Zangwill had performed "a great service to America by reminding us of the high hopes of the founders of the Republic."

IV

Yet even as audiences cheered *The Melting-Pot*, Zangwill's metaphor raised doubts. One had only to stroll around the great cities, as Basil March did in William Dean Howells's *A Hazard of New Fortunes*, to see that the melting process was incomplete. Ethnic minorities were forming their own *quartiers* in which they lived in their own way—not quite that of the lands they had left but not that of Anglocentric America either: Little Italy, Chinatown, Yorkville, Harlem, and so on.

Nor was the WASP culture showing great inclination to ease their access into Anglo-America. And when it did, when barriers fell, when new immigrants gained acceptance through money or celebrity, there loomed the prospect of intermarriage. In having his drama turn on marriage between people of different races and religions, Zangwill, who had himself married a Christian, emphasized where the melting pot must inexorably lead: to the submergence of separate ethnic identities in the new American race.

Was such a result desirable? Many immigrants doubtless thought so. In the early 20th century, most of their children certainly did. But soon ethnic spokesmen began to appear, moved by real concern for distinctive ethnic values and also by real if unconscious vested interest in the preservation of ethnic constituencies. Jewish reviewers castigated Zangwill: "All the worse for you and me, brother," wrote one, "who are to be cast into and dissolved in the crucible." Even some of Anglo-Saxon descent deplored the obliteration of picturesque foreign strains for the sake of insipid Anglocentric conformity.

The impression grew that the melting pot was a device to impose Anglocentric images and values upon hapless immigrants—an impression reinforced by the rise of the "Americanization" movement in response to the new polyglot immigration. Americanization programs, benign in intent, sought to expedite assimilation by offering immigrants special education in language, citizenship, and American history. The outbreak of war in 1914 gave Americanization a more coercive edge. Even presidents as friendly to immigrants as Theodore Roosevelt and Woodrow Wilson worried whether in crisis "hyphenated" Americans might not be more loyal to the old country than to their adopted land.

Three days after a German submarine sank the *Lusitania*, Wilson addressed an audience of recently naturalized citizens in Philadelphia. "You cannot become thorough Americans," he told them, "if you think of yourselves in groups. America does not consist of groups. A man who thinks of himself as belonging to a particular national group in America has not yet become an American."

"We can have no 'fifty-fifty' allegiance in this country," Theodore Roosevelt said two years later. "Either a man is an American and nothing else, or he is not an American at all." He condemned Americans who saw the world from the standpoint of another nation. "We Americans are children of the crucible," T. R. said. "The crucible does not do its work unless it turns out those cast into it in one national mould."

V

"One national mould"? Not everyone agreed. In 1915 Horace Kallen, a Jewish-American philosopher, wrote an essay for *The Nation* entitled "Democracy Versus the Melting-Pot." The melting pot, Kallen argued, was valid neither as a fact nor as an ideal. What impressed him was, on the contrary, the persistence of ethnic groups and their distinctive traditions. Unlike freely chosen affiliations, Kallen said, the ethnic bond was both involuntary and immutable. "Men may change their clothes, their politics, their wives, their religions, their philosophies, to a greater or lesser extent: they cannot change their grandfathers. Jews or Poles or Anglo-Saxons, in order to cease being Jews or Poles or Anglo-Saxons, would have to cease to be. . . ."

The Jewish-American philosopher Horace Kallen argued in 1915 that the concept of an American melting pot was a fallacy.

Ethnic diversity, Kallen observed, enriches American civilization. He saw the nation not as one people, except in a political and administrative sense, but rather "as a federation or commonwealth of national cultures . . . a democracy of nationalities, cooperating voluntarily and autonomously through common institutions . . . a multiplicity in a unity, an orchestration of mankind." This conception he came to call "cultural pluralism."

Kallen was unclear on the question of how to encourage ethnic separatism without weakening the original ideal of a single society. One critic warned that cultural pluralism would "result in the Balkanization of these United States." But Kallen made his attack on Anglo-centered assimilation at a time when critics of the melting pot could reasonably assume the solidity of the overarching framework. Because he considered political unity a given, he put his emphasis on the protection of cultural diversity.

The gospel of cultural pluralism was at first largely confined to academics, intellectuals, and artists. The postwar years saw much popular disenchantment with Europe, a Red Scare directed largely against aliens, the rise of the anti-Catholic Ku Klux Klan, and a campaign, realized in the Immigration Act of 1924, to freeze the ethnic composition of the American people. The new law established quotas on the basis of the national origins of the population in 1890, thereby drastically reducing the flow from southern and eastern Europe.

The xenophobic nationalism of the 1920s was followed in the 1930s by crises that, on some levels divisive, nevertheless strengthened the feeling that all Americans were in the same boat and might as well pull together. The Great Depression and the Second World War showed the desperate necessity of national cohesion within the frame of shared national ideals. "The principle on which this country was founded and by which it has always been governed," Franklin D. Roosevelt said in 1943, "is that Americanism is a matter of the mind and heart; Americanism is not, and never was, a matter of race and ancestry. A good American is one who is loyal to this country and to our creed of liberty and democracy."

VI

Gunnar Myrdal in 1944 showed no hesitation in declaring the American Creed the common possession of all Americans, even as his great book *An American Dilemma* provided a magistral analysis of America's most conspicuous failure to live up to the Creed: the treatment by white Americans of black America.

Noble ideals had been pronounced as if for all Americans, yet in practice they applied only to white people. Most interpretations of the national identity from Crèvecoeur on were for whites only. Even Horace Kallen, the champion of cultural pluralism, made no provision in his "democracy of nationalities" for black or red or brown or yellow Americans.

Tocqueville was an exception in factoring persons of color into the American equation. With his usual prescience, he identified racism as the irremediable flaw in American democracy. This "most grasping nation on the globe" had doomed the red man to extinction; and the presence of a black population was "the most formidable of all the ills that threaten the future of the Union." The more optimistic Emerson and Zangwill had thrown nonwhite nationalities into their smelting or melting pots, but Tocqueville saw racist exclusion as deeply ingrained in the national character.

History supported this judgment. White settlers had systematically pushed the American Indians back, killed their braves, seized their lands, and sequestered their tribes. They had brought Africans to America to work their plantations and Chinese to build their railroads. They had enunciated glittering generalities of freedom and withheld them from people of color. Their Constitution protected slavery, and their laws made distinctions on the basis of race. Though they eventually emancipated the slaves, they conspired in the reduction of the freedmen to third-class citizenship. Their Chinese Exclusion acts culminated in the total prohibition of Asian immigration in the Immigration Act of 1924. It occurred to damned few white Americans in these years that Americans of color were also entitled to the rights and liberties promised by the Constitution.

Yet what Bryce had called "the amazing solvent power" of American institutions and ideas retained its force, even among those most cruelly oppressed and excluded. Myrdal's polls of Afro-America showed the "determination" of blacks "to hold to the American Creed." Ralph Bunche, one of Myrdal's collaborators, observed that every man in the street—black, red, and yellow as well as white—regarded America as the "land of the free" and the "cradle of liberty." The American Creed, Myrdal surmised, meant even more to blacks than to whites, since it was the great means of pleading their unfulfilled rights. Blacks, new immigrants, Jews, and other disadvantaged groups, Myrdal said, "could not possibly have invented a system of political ideals which better corresponded to their interests."

The Second World War gave the Creed new bite. Hitler's racism forced Americans to look hard at their own racial assumptions. How, in fighting abroad against Hitler's doctrine of the Master Race, could Americans maintain a doctrine of white supremacy at home? How, with China a faithful American ally, could Americans continue to forbid Chinese to become American citizens? If the war did not end American racism, at least it drove much racial bigotry underground. The rethinking of racial issues challenged the conscience of the majority and raised the consciousness of minorities.

Emboldened by the Creed, blacks organized for equal opportunities in employment, opposed segregation in the armed forces, and fought in their own units on many fronts. After the war, the civil rights revolution, so long deferred, accelerated black self-reliance. So did the collapse of white colonialism around the world and the appearance of independent black states.

Across America minorities proclaimed their pride and demanded their rights. Women, the one "minority" that in America constituted a numerical majority, sought political and economic equality. Jews gained new solidarity from the holocaust and then from the establishment of a Jewish state in Israel. Changes in the immigration law dramatically increased the number arriving from Hispanic and Asian lands, and, following the general example, they asserted their own prerogatives. American Indians mobilized to reclaim rights and lands long since appropriated by the white man; their spokesmen even rejected the historic designation in which Indians had taken deserved pride and named themselves Native Americans.

The civil rights revolution provoked new expressions of ethnic identity by the now long-resident "new migration" from southern and eastern

Europe—Italians, Greeks, Poles, Czechs, Slovaks, Hungarians. The ethnic enthusiasm was reinforced by the "third-generation" effect formulated in Hansen's Law, named after Marcus Lee Hansen, the great pioneer in immigration history: "What the son wishes to forget the grandson wishes to remember."

Another factor powerfully nourished the passion for roots: the waning American optimism about the nation's prospects. For two centuries Americans had been confident that life would be better for their children than it was for them. In their exuberant youth, Americans had disdained the past and, as John Quincy Adams urged, looked forward to their posterity rather than backward to their ancestors. Amid forebodings of national decline, Americans now began to look forward less and backward more. The rising cult of ethnicity was a symptom of decreasing confidence in the American future.

VII

Ethnic as a word has had a long history. It originally meant "heathen" or "pagan" but soon came to mean anything pertaining to a race or nation. In this sense everyone, even the Lowells and the Cabots, were ethnics. By the time Henry James used the word in *The American Scene*, however, "ethnic" had acquired an association with foreignness. As applied since the 1960s, it definitely means non-Anglo minorities—a reversion to the original sense of being beyond the pale.

The noun *ethnicity* meanwhile made its modern debut in 1940 in W. Lloyd Warner's Yankee City series. From its modest beginning in that sociological study, "ethnicity" moved vigorously to center stage in popular discourse. The bicentennial of American independence, the centennial of the Statue of Liberty, the restoration of Ellis Island—all turned from tributes to the melting pot into extravaganzas of ethnic distinctiveness.

The pressure for the new cult of ethnicity came less from the minorities en masse than from their often self-appointed spokesmen. Most ethnics, white and nonwhite, saw themselves primarily as Americans. "The cravings for 'historical identity,'" Gunnar Myrdal said at the height of the ethnic rage, "is not in any sense a people's movement. Those cravings have been raised by a few well-established intellectuals, professors, writers—mostly, I gather, of a third generation." Few of them, Myrdal thought, made much effort to talk to their own ethnic groups. He feared, Myrdal added with a certain contempt, that this movement was only "upper-class intellectual romanticism."

Still, ideologues, with sufficient publicity and time, could create audiences. Spokesmen with a vested interest in ethnic identification turned against the ideal of assimilation. The melting pot, it was said, injured people by undermining their self-esteem. It denied them heroes—"role models," in the jargon—from their own ethnic ancestries. Praise now went to "the unmeltable ethnics."

In 1974, after testimony from ethnic spokesmen denouncing the melting pot as a conspiracy to homogenize America, Congress passed the Ethnic Heritage Studies Program Act—a statute that, by applying the ethnic ideology to all Americans, compromised the historic right of Americans to decide their ethnic identities for themselves. The act ignored those millions of Americans—surely a majority—who refused identification with any particular ethnic group.

The ethnic upsurge (it can hardly be called a revival because it was unprecedented) began as a gesture of protest against the Anglocentric culture. It became a cult, and today it threatens to become a counter-revolution against the original theory of America as "one people," a common culture, a single nation.

"Provides immediate relief from stress and anxiety."

Kelvin Dorch
Courier, Toronto, Canada

From pick-up to delivery, we can tell you within seconds exactly where on
Earth your shipment is. That's because, from the moment we receive it, your shipment is
entered into our worldwide tracking network with this SuperTracker® scanner, the
only device of its kind in the industry. It may be small, but it can take a big load off your mind.

HISTORY THE WEAPON

Writing history is an old and honorable profession with distinctive standards and purposes. The historian's goals are accuracy, analysis, and objectivity in the reconstruction of the past. But history is more than an academic discipline up there in the stratosphere. It also has its own role in the future of nations.

For history is to the nation rather as memory is to the individual. As an individual deprived of memory becomes disoriented and lost, not knowing where he has been or where he is going, so a nation denied a conception of its past will be disabled in dealing with its present and its future. As the means of defining national identity, history becomes a means of shaping history. The writing of history then turns from a meditation into a weapon. "Who controls the past controls the future," runs the Party slogan in George Orwell's *1984*; "who controls the present controls the past."

I

Historians do their damnedest to maintain the standards of their trade. Heaven knows how dismally we fall short of our ideals, how sadly our interpretations are dominated and distorted by unconscious preconceptions, how obsessions of race and nation blind us to our own bias. We remain creatures of our times, prisoners of our own experience, swayed hither and yon, like all sinful mortals, by partisanship, prejudice, dogma, by fear and by hope.

The spotlight we flash into the darkness of the past is guided by our own concerns in the present. When new preoccupations arise in our own times and lives, the spotlight shifts, throwing into sharp relief things that were always there but that earlier historians had casually excised from the collective memory. In this sense, the present may be said to re-create the past.

Historians must always strive toward the unattainable ideal of objectivity. But as we respond to contemporary urgencies, we sometimes exploit the past for nonhistorical purposes, taking from the past, or projecting upon it, what suits our own society or ideology. History thus manipulated becomes an instrument less of disinterested intellectual inquiry than of social cohesion and political purpose.

People live by their myths, and some may argue that the facts can be justifiably embroidered if embroiderment serves a higher good, such as the nurture of a nation or the elevation of a race. It may seem more important to maintain a beneficial fiction than to keep history pure—especially when there is no such thing as pure history anyway. This may have been what Plato had in mind when he proposed the idea of the "noble lie" in *The Republic.*

But enthusiasts are all too likely to confuse "noble lies" with reality. The corruption of history by nationalism is instructive. Nationalism remains, after two centuries, the most vital political emotion in the world—far more vital than social ideologies such as communism or fascism or even democracy. But it was not the product of spontaneous generation. "Nationalism is not the awakening of nations to self-consciousness," as Ernest Gellner has said; "it invents nations where they do not exist. . . . " Nationalism was developed by intellectuals in the interest of aspiring elites and thereafter propagated to receptive masses. And it continues to thrive because it taps potent emotions of history and locality to give individual lives meaning in an increasingly baffling universe.

Today the nationalist fever encircles the globe. In the West the contagion convulses Ireland and Israel, divides Belgium, Cyprus, and Canada, arouses Brittany, Corsica, and the Basque country. Nationalism broke up the Soviet empire and now threatens to break up the Soviet Union itself. In the third world, nationalism, having overthrown Western colonialism, launches a horde of new states, large and micro, often at each other's throats in reenacting ancient quarrels of history.

Within nation-states, nationalism takes the form of ethnicity or tribalism. In country after country across the third world—India, Burma, Sri Lanka, Indonesia, Iraq, Ethiopia, Nigeria, Angola, Trinidad, Guyana—ethnic groups struggle for power and, in desperate cases, for survival. The ethnic upsurge in America, far from being unique, partakes of the global fever.

II

The invocation of history is indispensable to nations and groups in the process of making themselves. How else can a people establish the legitimacy of its personality, the continuity of its tradition, the correctness of its course?

Often history is invoked to justify the ruling class. "The past," writes the British historian J. H. Plumb, "has always been the handmaid of authority." This is top-dog history, designed to show how noble, virtuous, and inevitable existing power arrangements are. Because it vindicates the status quo and the methods by which power is achieved and maintained, it may be called exculpatory history

Other times history is invoked to justify the victims of power, to vindicate those who reject the status quo. Isaiah Berlin has described how the "humiliated and defeated Germans" in the early 19th century lashed back against the arrogant French:

> They discovered in themselves qualities far superior to those of their tormentors. They contrasted their own deep, inner life of the spirit, their own profound humility, their selfless pursuit of true values—simple, noble, sublime—with the rich, worldly, successful, superficial, smooth, heartless, morally empty French. This mood rose to fever pitch during the national resistance to Napoleon, and was indeed the original exemplar of the reaction of many a backward, exploited, or at any rate patronised society, which, resentful of the apparent inferiority of its status, reacted by turning to real or imaginary triumphs and glories in its past, or enviable attributes of its own national or cultural character. . . . Hence the value of a real or imaginary rich historical past to inferiority-ridden peoples, for it promises, perhaps, an even more glorious future.

This is underdog history, designed to demonstrate what Bertrand Russell called the "superior virtue of the oppressed" by inventing or exaggerating past glories and purposes. It may be called compensatory history.

Both exculpatory and compensatory history use the past in order to shape the future. For 70 years in the Soviet Union, scholars practiced exculpatory history, sedulously defending every twist of the party line and every whim of the Kremlin dictatorship. Then came Gorbachev; and *glasnost* led in due course to the emancipation of historians.

For the first time ever, Soviet historians became free to write honest history—to describe the purges and the gulags, to demythologize Stalin and even Lenin, to reassess Bukharin and even Trotsky, to condemn the Soviet-Nazi pact of 1939, to pronounce Stalin's U.S.S.R. a totalitarian state, even to doubt the sacred Revolution itself. "A new future requires a new past," said Eric Foner of Columbia after four months as a lecturer at Moscow State University. "To legitimize these far-reaching changes, the press and public officials now paint the history of the Soviet era in the blackest hues." As party-line history was an instrument of dictatorship, honest history is an instrument of democracy.

In Japan the government's dedication to exculpatory history demonstrated persisting unwillingness to accept responsibility for aggressions and atrocities of half a century ago. School textbooks unrepentantly portray the Japanese conquest of Korea and invasion of China in terms so benevolent as to provoke official protests from Seoul and Beijing. Young Japanese are taught to see their country as a victim rather than the cause of the Pacific War.

When the eminent historian Professor Saburō Ienaga tried, as he wrote in the preface to the English edition of his notable book *The Pacific War*, "to show the Japanese people the naked realities," he was subjected to official persecution. Japanese courts upheld the Education Ministry's censorship of Ienaga's factual account of the Japanese "rape of Nanjing" in 1937. As Ienaga observed, the less the young people of Japan are taught the true history of the war, the greater the risk of a "similar danger" in years to come.

By the 1960s German historians had come to accept the crimes of Hitler as a unique German responsibility and to trace Nazism back to 19th-century German history and culture. But the revival of German nationalism in the 1980s set off a scholarly campaign to sanitize the national past. The crimes of Hitler, influential historians argued, were not unique, nor were they peculiarly German. All Hitler was doing was to imitate genocidal policies invented by Stalin, substituting race for class. Hitler had no doubt done awful things, but other nations had committed comparable atrocities without suffering the same international disfavor. Nazism was deplorable but not fundamental, more a matter of bad luck and aberration.

As Franz Josef Strauss, the conservative leader, said, Germans must not let the vision of their glorious past "be blocked by the sight-screens of those accursed 12 years between 1933 and 1945. German history cannot be presented as an endless chain of mistakes and crimes." Michael Stürmer, a conservative historian, criticizes the German "obsession with their guilt" and calls for a new affirmation of national identity. Stürmer understands the stakes: "Loss of orientation and the search for identity are brothers. . . . Anyone who believes that this has no effect on politics and the future ignores the fact that *in a land without history, he who fills the memory, defines the concepts, and interprets the past, wins the future.*"

History is a weapon. Perhaps their own vicissitudes as a nation—from democracy to Nazism to communism back to democracy in half a century—have made Czechs particularly sensitive to the manipulations of history. "The first step in liquidating a people," a historian observes in Milan Kundera's *The Book of Laughter and Forgetting*, "is to erase its memory. Destroy its books, its culture, its history. Then have somebody write new books, manufacture a new culture, invent a new history. Before long the nation will begin to forget what it is and what it was." "The struggle of man against power," says another character, "is the struggle of memory against forgetting."

Vaclav Havel, Czech playwright and president, made a pointed address in the presence of Kurt Waldheim of Austria. "He who fears facing his own past," Havel said, "must necessarily fear what lies before him. . . . Lying can never save us from the lie. Falsifiers of history do not safeguard freedom but imperil it. . . . Truth liberates man from fear." Honest history is the weapon of freedom.

III

American history was long written in the interests of white Anglo-Saxon Protestant males. My father, growing up in the 1890s in Xenia, a small Ohio town containing large contingents of Germans, Irish, and blacks, one day asked his father, who had come from Germany as a child and whose hero was Carl Schurz, the American army officer, politician, and reformer, why the schoolbooks portrayed England as the one and only mother country. My grandfather's wry comment was that apparently the only Germans worth mentioning were "the Hessians who had fought on the wrong side in the War for Independence." Irish and blacks fared even less well in schoolbooks, and the only good Indians were dead Indians. Non-WASPs were the invisible men (and women) in the American past.

The Anglocentric domination of schoolbooks was based in part on unassailable facts. For better or for worse, American history has been shaped more than anything else by British tradition and culture. Like it or not, as Andrew Hacker, the Queens political scientist, puts it, "For almost all this nation's history, the major decisions have been made by white Christian men." To deny this perhaps lamentable but hardly disputable fact would be to falsify history. But history can also be falsified by suppression of uglier aspects of Anglo rule—callous discrimination against later immigrants, brutal racism against nonwhite minorities—and by the creation of filiopietistic myths.

Myth-making began as early as Parson Weems's biography of Washington. As Anglocentric myths grew, they had at times to be protected against the British themselves. Anglophobia died slowly in the United States; and, despite the current theory of an Anglo-Saxon cultural conspiracy, American WASPs, from the Adamses in the 18th century to the Lodges in the 20th, were always among the leading Anglophobes.

After the First World War, patriotic organizations, persuaded that Britain had tricked the United States into the struggle, hunted down pro-British propaganda in American textbooks—as 30 years later a new generation of superpatriots hunted down pro-Soviet propaganda. Scholars were charged with selling out to British gold and plotting to bring the republic back into the empire. Official investigations were launched against "Anglicized" books in New York City, Washington, D.C., St. Louis, and elsewhere. Wisconsin, Oklahoma, and Oregon passed "pure-history" laws.

William Hale Thompson, running for mayor of Chicago in 1927 with the support of Colonel McCormick's Anglophobic *Chicago Tribune*, seized upon this agitation, promising to "biff King George on the snoot" if he dared come to Chicago. In his book *New Viewpoints in American History*, my father had an ironic sentence about the representatives of George V rendering homage "at the tomb of the great disloyalist and rebel of a former century, George Washington." Discovering *New Viewpoints* on a University of Chicago reading list, Big Bill Thompson denounced the "infamous book" and its infamous author for thus characterizing the sainted father of his country. A Thompson hench-man, a Damon Runyon character called Sport Herrmann, tried to remove the "treason-tainted" book from the public library. Frustrated there, Sport bought himself a copy and burned it in a patriotic bonfire.

An early cultural pluralist, Big Bill Thompson was determined not only to "stop the defamation of America's heroes" but to see that justice was done to "heroes of Irish, Polish, German, Holland, Italian, and other extractions." As ruling groups cherish their set of self-justifying myths, so excluded groups seek counter-affirmations of their own historical and cultural dignity, myths celebrating, and often exaggerating in the man-ner so well described by Isaiah Berlin, their own unacknowledged contributions to the making of America.

Big Bill Thompson was elected mayor of Chicago in 1927 on an anti-British platform, charging that British propa-ganda was written into American text-books to bring America back into the British Empire.

IV

The ethnic enclaves thus developed a compensatory literature. In-spired by group resentment and pride, this literature very often suc-cumbed to the Platonic temptation of "noble lies." Professor John V. Kelleher, Harvard's distinguished Irish-American scholar, provided gently satiric testimony about the Irish case:

> My earliest acquaintance with Irish-American history of the written variety was gained from the sort of articles that used to appear in minor Catholic magazines or in the Boston Sunday papers. They were turgid little essays on the fact that the Continental Army was 76 percent Irish, or that many of George Washington's closest friends were nuns or priests, or that Lincoln got the major ideas for the Second Inaugural Address from the Hon. Francis P. Mageghegan of Alpaca, New York, a pioneer manufacturer of cast-iron rosary beads.

This is what Professor Kelleher called the there's-always-an-Irishman-at-the-bottom-of-it-doing-the-real-work approach to American history.

Such ethnic chauvinism was largely confined, however, to tribal celebrations. Even in Boston and environs, where the Irish dominated school and library boards, they made no effort to impose their compen-satory history on the public-school curriculum. And as the Irish rose in

American society, Kelleher recalled, pietistic articles began to vanish from the Boston press. "Now one is rarely seen," he wrote in 1960, "even around March 17. I wonder whose is the major component in the Continental Army these days." (The answer would probably be blacks and Jews.) Kelleher was musing about the Irish in the spring of the year that an Irish Catholic was elected president of the United States—a signal of ultimate acceptance that relieved Irish-Americans of the need for ethnic cheerleading.

People from groups that began by sitting far beneath the salt may end, once they have made it themselves, by defending the Anglocentric canon. In 1990 Peggy Noonan, the charming and witty Irish-American ghostwriter for a second Irish-American president, urged that immigrants be instructed, not in the exploits of their own crowd, but in "the great unifying myths that define the dreams, characteristics, and special history of America. . . ." Otherwise, she said, "if our retelling of our past is dominated by the compulsive skepticism of the modern mind, with its ill-thought-out disdain, then we will stop being America."

Nor has anyone in recent years more wrathfully denounced scholarly iconoclasm than Professor Allan Bloom, the Jewish-American author of *The Closing of the American Mind*. "We are used to hearing the Founders charged with being racists, murderers of Indians, representatives of class interests," Professor Bloom wrote, condemning the debunkers for "weakening our convictions of the truth or superiority of American principles and our heroes."

Debunking is an ephemeral phenomenon, nothing to get excited about. If any kind of positive case can be made, rebunkers will appear in due course. The British historical journalist Paul Johnson can even make a hero out of Calvin Coolidge. History proceeds by revision and counterrevision. As the great Dutch historian Pieter Geyl splendidly put it, "History is indeed an argument without end."

Harvard professor John V. Kelleher referred to Irish compensatory literature of the 1960s as the "there's-always-an-Irishman-at-the-bottom-of-it-doing-the-real-work approach to American history."

V

The Irish and the Jews had their share of gristle in the American cauldron, but they finally made it: hence the emergence of people named Noonan and Bloom as defenders of Anglocentric verities. The situation is radically different for nonwhite minorities facing not snobbism but racism.

Most white Americans through most of American history simply considered colored Americans inferior and unassimilable. Not until the 1960s did integration become a widely accepted national objective. Even then, even after legal obstacles to integration fell, social, economic, and psychological obstacles remained. Blacks and Indians confront American democracy with its most tragic challenge.

Both black Americans and red Americans have every reason to seek redressment of the historical balance. Indians, however, lack the numbers, the unity, the visibility, and the political weight of African-Americans. Twelve percent of Americans are black, and the felt pressure to correct injustices of past scholarship comes mostly on their behalf. And indeed the cruelty with which white Americans have dealt with black Americans has been compounded by the callousness with which white historians have dealt with black history.

Even the best historians: Frederick Jackson Turner, dismissing the slavery question as a mere "incident" when American history is "rightly viewed"; Charles and Mary Beard in their famous *The Rise of American Civilization*, describing blacks as passive in slavery and ludicrous in Reconstruction and acknowledging only one black achievement—the invention of ragtime; Samuel Eliot Morison and Henry Steele Commager, writing about childlike and improvident Sambo on the old plantation. One can sympathize with W.E.B. Du Bois's rage after reading white histories of slavery and Reconstruction; he was, he wrote, "literally aghast at what American historians have done to this field . . . one of the most stupendous efforts the world ever saw to discredit human beings. . . . "

The job of redressing the balance has been splendidly undertaken in recent years by both white and black historians. Meticulous and convincing scholarship has reversed conventional judgments on slavery, on Reconstruction, on the role of the blacks in American life. After the murder of Medgar Evers in Mississippi in 1963, President Kennedy invited his widow and children to the White House. Later, Kennedy reflected on the days when Radical Republicans like Thaddeus Stevens advocated a tough Reconstruction policy toward the South. "I'm coming to believe that Thaddeus Stevens was right," he said. "I had always been taught to regard him as a man of vicious bias." He would not be taught that way today.

The reversal has extended from the world of scholarship to the popular culture. *Glory*, Edward Zwick's superb movie, told many white Americans for the first time about the record of black soldiers in the Civil War. How many had known before that 186,000 blacks served in the Union Army—about the same number as composed the entire United States Army in 1939?

But scholarly responsibility was only one factor behind the campaign of correction. History remains a weapon. "History's potency is mighty," Herbert Aptheker, the polemical chronicler of slave rebellions, has written. "The oppressed need it for identity and inspiration." (Aptheker, a faithful Stalinist, was an old hand at the manipulation of history.) "The thing that has kept most of us, that is, African-Americans, almost crippled in this society," said Malcolm X, "has been our complete lack of knowledge concerning the past."

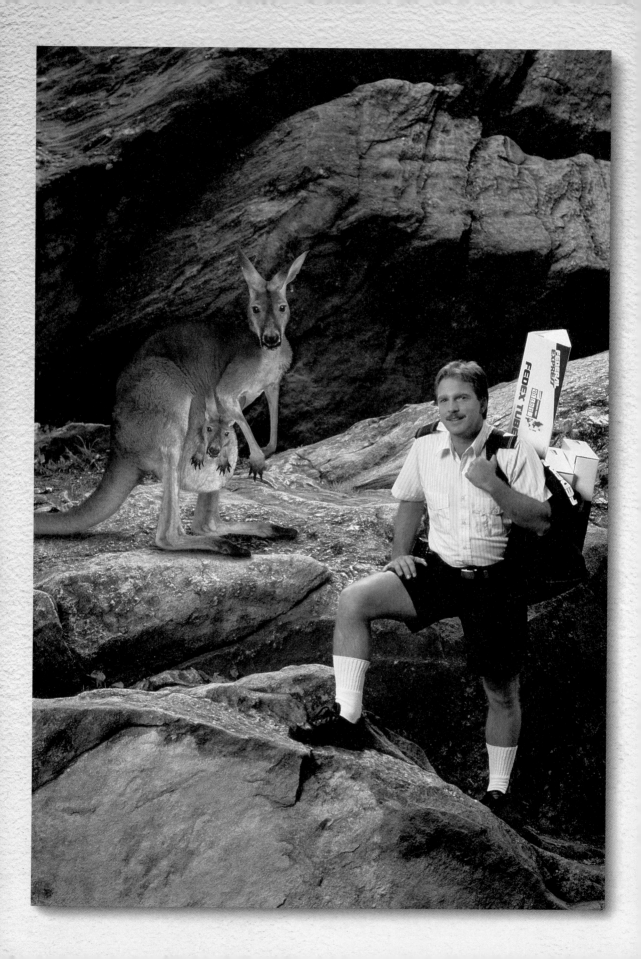

"Born to carry."

Matthew Gallagher
Courier, Sydney, Australia

Few carriers know the in's and out's of shipping Down Under the way we do
at Federal Express. Except, perhaps, for the one on the left.

More than Irish or Italians or Jews, black Americans, after generations of psychological and cultural evisceration, have every right to seek an affirmative definition of their past. Far more than white ethnics, they perceive themselves to be in a trap of cultural "hegemony" in which they are flooded by white values and demeaning self-images. Whites, some black intellectuals argue, control "knowledge production," and the need is to overcome "communicentric hegemony"—that is, "a canon which reflects the hegemonic culture." For blacks the American dream has been pretty much of a nightmare, and, far more than white ethnics, they are driven by a desperate need to vindicate their own identity.

"The academic and social rescue and reconstruction of Black history," as Maulana Karenga put it in his influential *Introduction to Black Studies* ("a landmark in the intellectual history of African Americans," according to Molefi Kete Asante of Temple University), "is . . . [an] indispensable part of the rescue and reconstruction of Black humanity. For history is the substance and mirror of a people's humanity in others' eyes as well as in their own eyes . . . not only what they have done, but also a reflection of who they are, what they can do, and equally important what they can become. . . ."

Activist-scholar Maulana Karenga contends that the rescue and reconstruction of black history are indispensable to the rescue and reconstruction of blacks.

VI

One can hardly be surprised at the emergence of a there's-always-a-black-man-at-the-bottom-of-it-doing-the-real-work approach to American history. A man named Crispus Attucks led the mob that British troops fired upon in the Boston Massacre before the Revolution and was among those killed. He was a sailor and of dark complexion, perhaps a mulatto, perhaps an Indian. No one knows much about Crispus Attucks. But "to evaluate a book on Attucks solely by the canons of scholarly objectivity and historical accuracy is missing the point," one writer observes. "It ignores the necessity of creating black counterparts to the Nathan Hales and Molly Pitchers of the white past."

Why this necessity? "The extent to which the past of a people is regarded as praiseworthy," the white anthropologist Melville J. Herskovits wrote in his study of the African antecedents of American blacks, "their own self-esteem would be high and the opinion of others will be favorable." The failure to celebrate the past, black publicists say today—as British and Irish and Jewish publicists had said before them—is a powerful reason for low self-esteem in the present. The remedy is the recovery of bygone glories and heroes. "We've got to stop waiting for white folks to put us in their history books," says Professor Jacob Gordon of the University of Kansas. "The Jews have done a good job of this. We've got to create Afrocentric academies and create our own history books."

White domination of American schools and colleges, black academics say, results in Eurocentric, racist, elitist, imperialist indoctrination and in systematic denigration of black values and achievements. "Physical enslavement," notes Kofi Lomotey of the State University of New York in Buffalo, has been succeeded by "psychological enslavement." "In the public-school system," writes Felix Boateng of Eastern Washington University, "the orientation is so Eurocentric that white students take their identity for granted, and African-American students are totally deculturalized"—deculturalization being the "process by which the individual is deprived of his or her culture and then conditioned to other cultural values." White education, writes Maulana Karenga, cuts out blacks, "the fathers and mothers of humankind and human civilization," and aims to turn black students into "obscene caricatures of Europe, pathetic imitators of their oppressors." Liberation would be impossible "until the white monopoly on Black minds was broken." "In a sense," says Molefi Kete Asante, the Eurocentric curriculum is "killing our children, killing their minds."

In history, Western-civilization courses are seen as cultural imperialism designed to disparage non-Western traditions and to impress the Western stamp on people of all races. In literature, the "canon," the accepted list of essential books, is seen as an instrumentality of the white power structure. Nowhere can blacks discover adequate reflection or representation of the black self. Black students, one scholar writes, "succumb to a sort of brainwashing which denies them the ego-strength that comes from self-awareness, self-knowledge, and the security of group identity." Asante advises black students to take two sets of notes—one to help them pass the examinations, the other to preserve their sanity. "When they say Shakespeare was the greatest writer who ever lived, you write it down so you can pass the test. But you write in the margins, 'This is nonsense.'"

Professor Asa Hilliard, who conceived a series of "African-American Baseline Essays," claims that Africa is the mother of Western civilization.

Some black educators even argue ultimate biological and mental differences, asserting that black students do not learn the way white students do and that the black mind works in a genetically distinctive way. Black children are said, in the jargon of the educationist, to "process information differently." "There are scientific studies that show, at early ages, the difference between Caucasian infants and African infants," says Clare Jacobs, a teacher in Washington, D.C. "Our African children are very expressive. Every thought we have has an emotional dimension to it, and Western education has historically subordinated the feelings." Charles Willie of Harvard finds several distinct "intelligences" of which the "communication and calculation" valued by whites constitute only two. Other kinds of "intelligence" are singing and dancing, in both of which blacks excel.

According to Professor Asa Hilliard, a black psychologist at Georgia State University, black students have cultural characteristics that whites lack: "high levels of energy, impulsive interrupting, and loud talking." (Hilliard's acquaintance with whites must be limited.) The "communication style" of the black child, writes another black psychologist, Na'im Akbar, includes considerable body language, eye movement, and positioning, "words that depend upon context for meaning and that have little meaning in themselves" and "a wide use of many coined interjections (sometimes profanity)." To force black children to learn standard English, some contend, only deepens their sense of inferiority; blacks should therefore be taught in "black English" as Hispanics should be taught in Spanish.

The psychological difference between blacks and whites, some hold, has an organic base. Whites must strive for supremacy, according to the black psychiatrist Frances Cress, to make up for their racial inferiority, caused by their "genetic inability to produce the skin pigments of melanin which are responsible for all skin coloration." "Black superiority in the areas of mental development, neurological functioning, and psychomotor development," opines Amos Wilson, "[are] . . . all related to the possession of a high level of melanin."

Salvation lies in breaking the white, Eurocentric, racist grip on the curriculum and providing education that responds to colored races, colored histories, colored ways of learning and behaving. Europe has reigned long enough; it is the source of most of the evil in the world anyway; and the time is overdue to honor the African contributions to civilization so purposefully suppressed in Eurocentric curricula. Children from nonwhite minorities, so long persuaded of their inferiority by the white hegemons, need the support and inspiration that identification with role models of the same color will give them.

The answer, for some at least, is "Afrocentricity," described by Asante in his book of that title as "the centerpiece of human regeneration." There is, Asante contends, a single "African Cultural System." Wherever people of African descent are, "we respond to the same rhythms of the universe, the same cosmological sensibilities. . . . Our Africanity is our ultimate reality." Those who say that Africans and African-Americans have nothing in common but the color of their skin are talking nonsense. "There exists an emotional, cultural, psychological connection . . . that spans the ocean." Civilization originated in the highlands of East Africa, and "our ancestors do in fact gather to inspire us and do bring us victory."

VII

The belated recognition of the pluralistic character of American society has had a bracing impact on the teaching and writing of history. The women's-liberation movement, the civil rights movement, the ethnic upsurge, and other forms of group self-assertion forced historians to look at old times in new ways. Scholars now explore such long-neglected fields as the history of women, of immigration, of blacks, Indians, Hispanics, and other minorities. Voices long silent ring out of the darkness of history.

The result has been a reconstruction of American history partly on the merits and partly in response to ethnic pressures. In 1987 the two states with both the greatest and the most diversified populations—California and New York—adopted new curricula for grades one to 12. Both state curricula materially increased the time allotted to non-European cultures.

The New York curriculum went further in minimizing Western traditions. A two-year global-studies course divided the world into seven regions—Africa, South Asia, East Asia, Latin America, the Middle East, Western Europe, and Eastern Europe—with each region given equal time. The history of Western Europe was cut back from a full year to one quarter of the second year. American history was reduced to a section on the Constitution; then a leap across Jefferson, Jackson, the Civil War, and Reconstruction to 1877.

In spite of the multiculturalization of the New York state history curriculum in 1987—a revision approved by such scholars as Eric Foner of Columbia and Christopher Lasch of Rochester—a newly appointed commissioner of education yielded to pressures from minority interests to consider still further revision. In 1989, a Task Force on Minorities: Equity and Excellence (not one historian among its 17 members) brought in a report, its first sentence sounding the keynote:

> African-Americans, Asian-Americans, Puerto Ricans/Latinos and Native Americans have all been the victims of an intellectual and educational oppression that has characterized the culture and institutions of the United States and the European American world for centuries.

The "systematic bias toward European culture and its derivatives," the report asserts, has "a terribly damaging effect on the psyche of young people of African, Asian, Latino, and Native American descent." The dominance of "the European-American monocultural perspective" explains why "large numbers of children of non-European descent are not doing as well as expected." The 1987 curriculum revision, the report concedes, did include more material on minority groups, but "merely adding marginal examples of 'other' cultures to an assumed dominant culture" cannot counteract "deeply rooted racist traditions"; all it produces is "Eurocentric multiculturalism."

Dr. Leonard Jeffries, the task force's consultant on African-American culture and a leading author of the report, discerns "deep-seated pathologies of racial hatred" even in the 1987 curriculum. A provocative

Professor Leonard Jeffries of City College of New York discerns "deep-seated pathologies of racial hatred" in curricula and describes Europeans as cold, individualist, materialistic, and aggressive "ice people."

teacher at the City College of New York, Jeffries describes Europeans as cold, individualistic, materialistic, and aggressive "ice people" who grew up in caves and have brought the world the three D's, "domination, destruction, and death," whereas Africans who grew up in sunlight, with the intellectual and physical superiority provided by melanin, are warm, humanistic, and communitarian "sun people." (He also tells his CCNY classes that "rich Jews" financed the slave trade.)

The consultant on Asian-American culture called for more pictures of Asian-Americans. The consultant on Latino culture found damning evidence of ethnocentric bias in such white usages as the Mexican War and the Spanish-American War. The ethnically correct designations should be the American-Mexican War and the Spanish-Cuban-Ameri-

can War. A later commentator objected to the term *slaves* on the ground
that it "depersonalizes the oppression of a people. If a text were to use
'enslaved persons,' the act of enslavement would be made more explicit."
The consultant on Native American culture wanted more space for
Indians and for bilingual education in Iroquois.

A new curriculum giving the four other cultures equitable treatment,
the report concluded, would provide "children from Native American,
Puerto Rican/Latino, Asian American, and African American cultures . . . higher self-esteem and self-respect, while children from European cultures will have a less arrogant perspective."

The report views division into racial groups as the basic analytical
framework for an understanding of American history. Its interest in
history is not as an intellectual discipline but rather as social and psychological therapy whose primary function is to raise the self-esteem of
children from minority groups. Nor does the report regard the Constitution or the American Creed as means of improvement. Jeffries scorns
the Constitution, finding "something vulgar and revolting in glorifying
a process that heaped undeserved rewards on a segment of the population while oppressing the majority." The belief in the unifying force of
democratic ideals finds no echo in the report, no doubt because the ideals
were disqualified by their Eurocentric origin. Indeed, the report takes
no interest in the problem of holding a diverse republic together. Its
impact is rather to sanction and deepen racial tensions.

VIII

The recent spread of Afrocentric programs to public schools represents an extension of the New York task-force ideology. These programs are in most cases based on a series of "African-American Baseline
Essays" conceived by the educational psychologist Asa Hilliard.

Hilliard's narration for the slide show "Free Your Mind, Return to the
Source: The African Origin of Civilization" suggests his approach.
"Africa," he writes, "is the mother of Western civilization"—an argument turning on the contention that Egypt was a black African country
and the real source of the science and philosophy Western historians
attribute to Greece. Africans, Hilliard continues, also invented birth
control and carbon steel. They brought science, medicine, and the arts to
Europe; indeed, many European artists, such as Browning and Beethoven, were in fact "Afro-European." They also discovered America long
before Columbus, and the original name of the Atlantic Ocean was the
Ethiopian Ocean.

Hilliard's African-American Baseline Essays were introduced into the
school system of Portland, Oregon, in 1987. They have subsequently
been the inspiration for Afrocentric curricula in Milwaukee, Indianapolis, Pittsburgh, Washington, D.C., Richmond, Atlanta, Philadelphia,

Detroit, Baltimore, Camden, and other cities and continue at this writing to be urged on school boards and administrators anxious to do the right thing.

John Henrik Clarke's Baseline Essay on Social Studies begins with the proposition that "African scholars are the final authority on Africa." Egypt, he continues, "gave birth to what later became known as Western civilization, long before the greatness of Greece and Rome." "Great civilizations" existed throughout Africa, where "great kings" ruled "in might and wisdom over vast empires." After Egypt declined, magnificent empires arose in West Africa, in Ghana, Mali, Songhay—all marked by the brilliance and enlightenment of their administration and the high quality of their libraries and universities. Then Moorish invaders from the north plundered the black empires and sent West Africa into decline. European slave traders thereafter invented "fantastic tales of savagery about Africans" so that the slave trade would appear an act of Christian charity. Clarke concedes that slavery existed in West Africa before the Europeans arrived, but it was, he suggests, a humane and kindly servitude. The subsequent deterioration of Africa was caused by "the greed and imperialistic goals of the European nations."

Professor John Henrik Clarke blames "the greed and imperialistic goals of the European nations" for the deterioration of Africa.

Other Baseline Essays argue in a similar vein that Africa was the birthplace of science, mathematics, philosophy, medicine, and art, and that Europe stole its civilization from Africa and then engaged in "malicious misrepresentation of African society and people . . . to support the enormous profitability of slavery." "It was not done by accident," adds Leonard Jeffries. "It was done as part of a conspiracy to prevent us from having a unified experience." The coordinator of multicultural/multi-ethnic education in Portland even says that Napoleon deliberately shot off the nose of the Sphinx so that the Sphinx would not be recognized as African.

Like other excluded groups before them, black Americans invoke supposed past glories to compensate for real past and present injustices. Because their exclusion has been more tragic and terrible than that of white immigrants, their quest for self-affirmation is more intense and passionate. In seeking to impose Afrocentric curricula on public schools, for example, they go further than their white predecessors. And belated recognition by white America of the wrongs so viciously inflicted on black Americans has created the phenomenon of white guilt—not a bad thing in many respects, but still a vulnerability that invites cynical black exploitation and manipulation.

The black American predicament is another variation on the familiar theme of nationalism. No American scholar has written more fondly about the Arab quest for identity or has more sharply accused the West of imperialism and racism than the Palestinian-American Edward W. Said of Columbia. Yet Said sees in his beloved Arab Middle East the pathos of "an aggrieved and unfulfilled nationalism, beset with conspiracies." He warns against "the provincial and self-pitying posture that argues that a largely fictional and monolithic West disdains us. . . . There are many Wests, some antagonistic, some not." He warns too against "thinkers who want to start from scratch and zealously, not to say furiously, take things back to some pure, sacred origin. This has given all sorts of pathologies time and space enough to take hold." Serious black scholars see the black predicament with similar clarity.

History as a weapon is an abuse of history. The high purpose of history is not the presentation of self nor the vindication of identity but the recognition of complexity and the search for knowledge. "We need odes not to blood and mythology or uprooted, mourned or dead plants," writes Said, "but to living creatures and actual situations."

"Every day, I help the world's most stylish women get dressed."

Jeffrey Spiegel
Worldwide Account Executive, New York City

PartsBank®, the Federal Express warehousing, inventory control, and distribution service,
allows designers to bring their latest creations in from Europe, into
the finest stores, in just days. Giving retailers priceless extra days to sell them.

THE BATTLE OF THE SCHOOLS

There is nothing more natural than for black Americans, as wounded racial groups have done through history, to assert pride and claim identity and, because black wounds are so much deeper than white, to do so with tragic intensity. Nor is there anything more natural than for generous-hearted people, black and white, to go along with Afrocentrism out of a decent sympathy for the insulted and injured of American society and of a decent concern to bind up the wounds. Still, doctrinaire ethnicity in general and the dogmatic black version in particular raise questions that deserve careful and dispassionate examination.

I

Cultural pluralism is a necessity in an ethnically diversified society. But the motives behind curriculum reform sometimes go beyond the desire for a more honest representation of the past. "Multiculturalism" arises as a reaction against Anglo- or Eurocentrism; but at what point does it pass over into an ethnocentrism of its own? The very word, instead of referring as it should to all cultures, has come to refer only to non-Western, nonwhite cultures. The president of the Modern Language Association even wonders why "we cannot be students of Western culture and multiculturalism at the same time." Can any historian justify the proposition that the five ethnic communities into which the New York state task force wishes to divide the country had equal influence on the development of the United States? Is it a function of schools to teach ethnic and racial pride? When does obsession with differences begin to threaten the idea of an overarching American nationality?

I am constrained to feel that the cult of ethnicity in general and the Afrocentric campaign in particular do not bode well either for American education or for the future of the republic. I would like to pose some of the questions that worry me.

Little is harder to talk honestly about in America these days than race.

Too many sensitivities are involved, too many opportunities for misunderstanding. I may perhaps be pardoned if I try to make clear where I come from. Both by inheritance and by conviction I believe in the pluralistic approach to the writing and teaching of history. My father was his generation's great champion of social history, of urban history, and immigration history. He was an active member—in the end, the last white member—of the executive council of the Association for the Study of Negro Life and History and a staunch friend of its director, the noted black historian Carter G. Woodson, and of such other black scholars as Charles Wesley, W. M. Brewer, Rayford W. Logan, Alruthius Taylor, and John Hope Franklin.

As for me, I was for a time a member of the executive council of the *Journal of Negro History*. I wrote in that journal 20 years ago that black history is "essential if we are to know in its majesty and terror the real history of the United States." I believe in the importance of teaching Americans the history of other cultures—East Asia, Latin America, the Middle East, Africa, Polynesia. I have been a lifelong advocate of civil rights.

Cultural pluralism is not the issue. Nor is the teaching of Afro-American or African history the issue; of course these are legitimate subjects. The issue is the kind of history that the New York task force, the Portland Baseline essayists, and other Afrocentric ideologues propose for American children. The issue is the teaching of *bad* history under whatever ethnic banner.

One argument for organizing a school curriculum around Africa is that black Africa is the birthplace of science, philosophy, religion, medicine, technology, of the great achievements that have been wrongly ascribed to Western civilization. But is this in fact true? Many historians and anthropologists regard Mesopotamia as the cradle of civilization; for a recent discussion, see Charles Keith Maisels' *The Emergence of Civilization*. If there were as many Iraqi-Americans as there are black Americans, we would no doubt have a campaign for an Iraqocentric curriculum—a campaign that could mobilize more substantial historical evidence than Afrocentrists have produced. But there aren't enough Iraqi-Americans, and by 1990 they had troubles of their own.

The Afrocentrist case rests largely on the proposition that ancient Egypt was essentially a black African country. I am far from being an expert on Egyptian history, but neither, one must add, are the educators and psychologists who push Afrocentrism. A book they often cite is Martin Bernal's *Black Athena*, a vigorous effort by a Cornell professor to document Egyptian influence on ancient Greece. In fact Bernal makes no very strong claims about Egyptian pigmentation; but, citing Herodotus, he does argue that several Egyptian dynasties "were made up of pharaohs whom one can usefully call black."

Frank M. Snowden Jr., the distinguished black classicist at Howard University and author of *Blacks in Antiquity*, is most doubtful about painting ancient Egypt black. Bernal's assumption that Herodotus meant black in the 20th-century sense is contradicted, Snowden demonstrates, "by Herodotus himself and the copious evidence of other classical authors." Frank J. Yurco, an Egyptologist at Chicago's Field Museum of Natural History, after examining the evidence derivable from mummies, paintings, statues, and reliefs, concludes in the *Biblical Archaeological Review* that ancient Egyptians, like their modern descendants, varied in color from the light Mediterranean type to the darker brown of upper Egypt to the still darker shade of the Nubians around Aswan. He adds that ancient Egyptians would have found the question meaningless and wonders at our presumption in assigning "our primitive racial labels" to so impressive a culture.

Yurco's verdict on John Henrik Clarke's Baseline Essay exposition of the Afrocentric case is comprehensive—"a mélange of misinformation, inconsistance [*sic*], outright fallacious information, half-truths, and outdated information . . . virtually valueless as scholarship . . . reads more like a medieval chronicle in parts than like a current survey of history."

The Egyptologist Dr. Miriam Lichtheim is equally dismissive: "I do not wish to waste any of my time refuting the errant [*sic*] nonsense which is being propagated in the American black community about the Egyptians being Nubians and the Nubians being black. The Egyptians were not Nubians, and the original Nubians were not black. Nubia gradually became black because black peoples migrated northward out of central Africa. The 'Nile Valley School' is obviously an attempt by American blacks to provide themselves with an ancient history linked to that of the high civilisation of ancient Egypt." "Totally false," says Professor Afaf Marsot of the Near-East Center of the University of California at Los Angeles. "That's a myth, based on the flimsiest kind of evidence. The Egyptians were a mixed population, as all Mediterranean people are mixed. Every Egyptologist will tell you what I'm telling you."

Arthur Schlesinger Jr., pictured here in 1958 with his father at Harvard University, has by "inheritance and by conviction" followed his father's pluralistic approach to the writing and teaching of history.

II

After Egypt, Afrocentrists teach children about the glorious West African emperors, the vast lands they ruled, the civilization they achieved; not, however, about the tyrannous authority they exercised, the ferocity of their wars, the tribal massacres, the squalid lot of the common people, the captives sold into slavery, the complicity with the Atlantic slave trade, the persistence of slavery in Africa after it was abolished in the West.

As for tribalism, the word *tribe* hardly occurs in the Afrocentric lexicon; but who can hope to understand African history without understanding the practices, loyalties, rituals, blood-feuds of tribalism? Black historians of an earlier generation, like Carter Woodson, wrote of the "orgies of war and sacrifice of human beings" in West African societies. That note is not struck in the Afrocentric curriculum.

One can go on indefinitely citing dubious claims Afrocentrist ideologues represent as facts—that Pythagoras and Aristotle, for example, stole their mathematics and philosophy from black scholars in Egypt. But there is no reliable evidence that either Pythagoras or Aristotle ever visited Egypt. In the case of Pythagoras, writes Professor L. Pearce Williams, the Cornell historian of science, the Babylonians and Egyptians certainly were acquainted with the Pythagorean relationship, but the Pythagorean theorems, the proof of the relationship, were Hellenic. In the case of Aristotle, the notion that Alexander the Great pillaged the Library of Alexandria on his old tutor's behalf falls before the facts that there was no Alexandria to pillage until Alexander founded the city and that the consensus of classical scholars is that the library was not established until half a century after Alexander and Aristotle died. In any case, ideas can hardly be "stolen"—totally removed from the original owner—like jewels. As Diane Ravitch sensibly asks, how in the world does one "lose knowledge by sharing it"?

The Baseline Essay on science and technology contains biographies of black American scientists, among them Charles R. Drew, who first developed the process for the preservation of blood plasma. In 1950 Drew, grievously injured in an automobile accident in North Carolina, lost quantities of blood. "*Not one* of several nearby white hospitals," according to the Baseline Essay, "would provide the blood transfusions he so desparately [*sic*] needed, and on the way to a hospital that treated Black people, he died." It is a hell of a story—the inventor of blood-plasma storage dead because racist whites denied him his own invention. Only it is not true. According to the biographical entry for Drew written by the eminent black scholar Rayford Logan of Howard for the *Dictionary of American Negro Biography*, "Conflicting versions to the contrary, Drew received prompt medical attention."

Is it really a good idea to teach minority children myths—at least to teach myths as facts? A reporter for the *Oregonian* describes what is going on these days in Portland classrooms: "[black students] have learned, for example, that Africans visited the Americas long before Columbus did and that Cleopatra was black." Is Afrocentric chauvinism any different from the Irish-American myth-making satirized by John V. Kelleher? Does not this uncritical glorification carry us back to Plato's "noble lies"?

III

The deeper reason for the Afrocentric campaign lies in the theory that the purpose of history in the schools is essentially therapeutic: to build a sense of self-worth among minority children. Eurocentrism, by denying nonwhite children any past in which they can take pride, is held to be the cause of poor academic performance. Race consciousness and group pride are supposed to strengthen a sense of identity and self-respect among nonwhite students.

Everyone is distressed over the state of American education, especially in our cities. Everyone is concerned with the search for remedies, especially remedies that will neither require money nor increase taxes. Curriculum revision costs little; it appeases militant nonwhite minorities; it relieves guilt feelings among the white majority. It might even work. Or will it? Does Afrocentrism have much possibility of working even in its own terms?

Will black children really do better in school if they are taught that everything good in the world came out of Africa? This proposition assumes a live connection between black America and Africa, and especially Egypt as Afrocentrism's prime exhibit. But any relationship between Egyptians, whatever color they may have been, and black Americans is exceedingly tenuous.

Black Americans do not trace their roots to Egypt. The great majority of their ancestors came from West Africa, especially the Guinea coast. They were from a variety of tribes and spoke a variety of languages; Professor Ali Mazrui tells us that Africa contains some 850 distinct ethnic and linguistic groups. Any homogeneity among slaves derived not from the African tribe but from the American plantation.

But what about Afrocentricity and the proposition that the black mind works in a genetically different way? May there not be abiding psychological and biological ties to Africa? The "unique status" of black psychology, claims the black psychologist Wade Nobles, derives from "basic African philosophy which dictates the values, customs, attitudes, and behavior of Africans in Africa and the New World." This line of thought has obvious affinities with Léopold Senghor's concept of Negritude, which in its original formulation saw blacks everywhere as genetically endowed with distinctive human values, psychological makeup, and cultural style. "Emotion is Negro," said Senghor, "as reason is Hellenic."

But unless one is to yield to biological determinism and accept that the possession of black skin creates a unique black mentality and character, it is hard to see what living connection exists between American blacks today and their heterogeneous West African ancestors three centuries ago. And biological determinism—the theory that race determines mentality—is of course just another word for racism. Biological determinism is exactly the theory apologists for slavery used in the American South before the Civil War. It is ironic to hear blacks using the same theory today.

Until very recent times, few black Americans have regarded the African connection as a major theme in their lives. David Walker, in his

1829 *Appeal . . . to the Colored Citizens of the World*, said of America, "This land which we have watered with our *tears* and our *blood* is now our mother country." The great Frederick Douglass on occasion invoked the glorious past in Africa but did so in order to vindicate racial equality in America. In "The Future of the Colored Race," an 1886 essay, Douglass "virtually repudiated," as Professor Wilson J. Moses, director of Afro-American Studies at Boston University, puts it, "any African identity." When the freedmen after emancipation chose last names, they took not African names but the names of American heroes—Washington, Jefferson, Jackson, Clay, Lincoln. "Centuries of residence, centuries of toil, centuries of suffering have made us Americans," a black high-school principal in Ohio said in 1874. "In language, in civilization, in fears, and in hopes we are Americans."

"Neither my father nor my father's father ever saw Africa," recalled W.E.B. Du Bois, "or knew its meaning or cared overmuch for it." His own black associates in the National Association for the Advancement of Colored People, Du Bois recalled, had a "fierce repugnance toward anything African. . . . They felt themselves Americans, not Africans. They resented and feared any coupling with Africa." Though Du Bois himself spent his last years in West Africa, he had earlier dismissed the African connection: "Once for all, let us realize that we are Americans, that we were brought here with the earliest settlers and that the very sort of civilization from which we came made the complete absorption of Western modes and customs imperative if we were to survive all; in brief, *there is nothing so indigenous, so completely 'made in America' as we.*"

W.E.B. Du Bois (1868-1963), black historian, sociologist, novelist, editor, and activist, said in 1800, "The problem of the 20th century is the problem of the color line."

From time to time, black leaders, notably Martin Delany in the mid-19th century and Marcus Garvey in the 1920s, excited passing interest in Africa. But Delany's campaign was derailed by the Civil War, and Garvey was a Jamaican who developed his back-to-Africa vision in England; his American influence was short-lived. Mussolini's attack on Ethiopia in 1935 set off another spasm of interest, again short-lived.

I recall the 1956 presidential campaign. Adlai Stevenson, for whom I was working, had a weak record on civil rights in America but a strong record on nationalism in Africa. I suggested to a group of sympathetic black leaders that maybe if Stevenson talked to black audiences about Africa for the Africans, he could make up for his deficiencies on civil rights. My friends laughed and said that American blacks couldn't care less about Africa.

"Nor can the American Negro," wrote Abram L. Harris, the radical black economist, "be considered in any logical way African." The black educator Horace Mann Bond spoke in 1959 of "the American Negro's traditional aversion to Africa and things African." In 1964 the sociologist Milton Gordon wrote about black Americans, "Their sense of identification with ancestral African national cultures is virtually nonexistent."

"The Negro is an American," Martin Luther King Jr. told Robert Penn Warren. "We know nothing of Africa."

Countee Cullen's poem sums it up:

What is Africa to me:
Copper sun or scarlet sea,
Jungle star or jungle track,
Strong bronzed men, or regal black
Women from whose loins I sprang
When the birds of Eden sang?

One three centuries removed
From the scenes his fathers loved,
Spicy grove, cinnamon tree,
What is Africa to me?

IV

Obviously attitudes toward Africa have changed markedly in the last 25 years. But American Afrocentrism is really a case of what the English historian Eric Hobsbawm calls "the invention of tradition." Alex Haley's compelling *Roots* helped create an audience for the tradition—though, as Ishmael Reed later observed, if Haley had traced his father's rather than his mother's bloodline, "he would have traveled 12 generations back to, not Gambia, but *Ireland.*"

The great stimulus was less the civil rights revolution, which had rushed along without benefit of Afrocentrism, than it was the pride generated by the appearance of independent African states—for many American blacks a proof of racial virility, as the establishment of Israel was for many American Jews. The analogy is incomplete. Where Jewish-Americans can (or could until recently) look with pride on the achievements of Israel, African-Americans, hard put to find much to admire in contemporary Liberia or Uganda or Ghana, must instead seek moments of glory in the dim past.

The glorification of the African past was accompanied by a campaign to replace Anglo "slave" names with African names, to wear African costumes, to replicate African rituals. LeRoi Jones, who had said in 1962 that "history for the Negro, before America, must remain an emotional abstraction," now saw Africa more concretely and changed his name to Amiri Baraka. Arthur Smith became Molefi Kete Asante and called on others to embrace African names: "only such a name reflects our consciousness."

At Asa Hilliard's conference "Infusion of African and African-American Content in the School Curriculum," John Henrik Clarke was honored by the Ashanti Enstoolment ceremony: first, the blowing of a shell-horn and the beating of drums, then the lowering of Clarke three times onto the seat of respect. "Five bare-chested men in sashes, with gold bangles around their heads, paraded in," reports Andrew Sullivan in *The New Republic*, "carrying a vast yellow parasol topped by a small ivory elephant."

In another session Abena Walker said that Afrocentric education in the District of Columbia would lean heavily on ritual, music, and mantras; children would "learn through rhythm and rapping." Wade Nobles, dressed in a lilac-blue robe, carried to the podium a fetish to ward off evil and observed the African custom of seeking the permission of elders before beginning to speak. "When we adopt other people's theories," he proceeded to say, "we are like Frankenstein [he meant Frankenstein's monster] doing other people's wills. It's like someone drinking some good stuff, vomiting it, and then we have to catch the vomit and drink it ourselves. . . . Don't become the vomit-drinkers!"

Surely there is something a little sad about all this—quite beyond the vulgar outburst that dismisses the European intellectual heritage as vomit. There is little evidence, however, that such invention of tradition is much more than the pastime of a few angry, ambitious, and perhaps despairing zealots and hustlers. Their impact is greater on the guilt of whites than on the common sense of the black community.

The Africanization of black Americans has not got very far. Perhaps this is because, as the black historian Nathan Huggins has written, "An Afro-American and the grandson of a Polish immigrant will be able to take more for granted between themselves than the former could with a Nigerian or the latter with a Warsaw worker." As even Asante concedes, when black Americans visit Africa, Africans perceive them as plain Americans and hardly as African at all.

Washington Post columnist William Raspberry contends that Afrocentric education will make black children "less competent in the culture in which they have to compete."

Anyone who knows anything about Africa, the black columnist William Raspberry of *The Washington Post* has written, knows that there is no single "African" culture from which black Americans are descended. "While some Africans were establishing a university at Timbuktu, others were engaged in slavery or tribal warfare or cannibalism. Some Africans were monotheists, while others were animists. As with their European counterparts, some were promoting brilliant philosophies, while others were savages." As for the Afrocentric curriculum, Raspberry adds, it is a "questionable assumption that black children, with only the vaguest notions of their African ancestry, can be inculcated with African culture more easily than the American culture to which they are daily exposed."

The fate of the campaign to replace "black" with "African-American" is instructive. "To be called black," Jesse Jackson has said, "is baseless. . . . To be called African-American has cultural integrity." The term *Afro-American* has indeed been used intermittently in the United

"Our planes may deliver the shipments. But I deliver the planes."

Jim Simmons
Lead Mechanic, Chicago

One reason why our planes do such an outstanding job is because
our mechanics do such an outstanding job. In fact, over the years, we've managed
to maintain an on-time performance record that's the envy of every scheduled airline.
Which explains why nobody delivers like Federal Express.

States since the 1850s, but it has never quite caught on, and black Americans are not rushing to embrace the hyphen now. A *Washington Post*-ABC poll in 1990 showed 66 percent favoring "black" over "African-American"; a 1991 survey by the Joint Center for Political and Economic Studies, a research organization specializing in black issues, found the vote 72 percent to 15 percent in favor of "black."

V

Even if black America had a spontaneous and authentic relationship with Africa, would learning about Africa improve the self-esteem of black children?

The New York curricular-revision task force claims that the monocultural Eurocentric bias has "a terribly damaging effect on the psyche of young people of African, Asian, Latino, and Native American descent." The idea that Europe has produced one homogeneous culture seems rather weird. What is so "monocultural" about the wild mix of people from Reykjavík to Athens and from Lisbon to Omsk? Can Henry Adams and the person he once described as "a furtive Yacoob or Ysaac still reeking of the Ghetto, snarling a weird Yiddish to the officers of the customs" be usefully regarded as products of a single culture? Churchill and Hitler, St. Francis and Machiavelli, Pericles and Dracula—monocultural?

In any event, the task-force report vouchsafes no proof for the assertion that a Eurocentric bias wrecks the psyches of minority children. So far as I can find out, there is no scientific study showing any correlation between ethnic-studies programs and the self-esteem of ethnic groups. Asked whether the Afrocentric curriculum would improve the performance of minority children, even Asa Hilliard sounds uncertain: "I don't know that anyone has done the research to be able to say, other than by impression and opinion, what's going to happen."

The theory is that immersion in the history of one's own group will overcome feelings of racial inferiority both by instilling pride in past ethnic accomplishments and by providing ethnic role models to inspire future performance. Telling black children how marvelous old Africa was will make them work harder and do better. But does study of the glory that was Greece and the grandeur that was Rome improve the academic record of Greek-American and Italian-American children? Not so that anyone has noticed. Why is it likely to help black children, who are removed from their geographical origins not by 50 years but by 300?

Nor does the absence of historical role models seem to have handicapped two other groups in American society—Jewish-Americans and Asian-Americans. Nor are there Semitocentric or Asiacentric public-school curricula glorifying the civilization of their ancestors. Yet Jewish-Americans and even more particularly Asian-Americans—3 percent of the population, 30 percent of the students at Berkeley—have academic success out of proportion to their numbers in the population.

Why does anyone suppose that pride and inspiration are available only from people of the same ethnicity? Can only relatives be role models? Plainly this is not the case. At the age of 12, Frederick Douglass encountered a book entitled *The Columbian Orator* containing speeches by Burke, Sheridan, Pitt, and Fox. "Every opportunity I got," Douglass later said, "I used to read this book." The orations "gave tongue to interesting thoughts of my own soul, which had frequently flashed through my mind, and died away for want of utterance. . . . What I got from Sheridan was a bold denunciation of slavery and a powerful vindication of human rights. The reading of these documents enabled me to utter my thoughts." Douglass did not find the fact that the orators were white an insuperable obstacle.

Nor did W.E.B. Du Bois shrink from contact with the Eurocentric tradition. "I sit with Shakespeare and he winces not. Across the color line I move arm in arm with Balzac and Dumas, where smiling men and welcoming women glide in gilded halls. . . . I summon Aristotle and Aurelius and what soul I will, and they come all graciously with no scorn nor condescension. So, wed with Truth, I dwell above the veil."

Or hear Ralph Ellison: "In Macon County, Alabama, I read Marx, Freud, T. S. Eliot, Pound, Gertrude Stein, and Hemingway. Books which seldom, if ever, mentioned Negroes were to release me from whatever 'segregated' idea I might have had of my human possibilities." He was freed, Ellison continued, not by the example of Richard Wright and other black writers but by artists who offered a broader sense of life and possibility. "It requires real poverty of the imagination to think that this can come to a Negro only through the example of other Negroes." As he added many years later, when the black writer Charles Johnson won the National Book Award for *Middle Passage*, "You don't write out of your skin, for God's sake, you write out of your imagination."

When Sterling Brown, Arthur P. Davis, and Ulysses Lee brought out their influential anthology of black writing, *The Negro Caravan*, in 1941, they disclaimed the notion that black writing falls "into a unique cultural pattern. . . . Many contemporary Negro writers are closer to O. Henry, Carl Sandburg, Edgar Lee Masters, Edna St. Vincent Millay, Waldo Frank, Ernest Hemingway, and John Steinbeck than to each other. The bonds of literary tradition seem to be stronger than race."

Martin Luther King Jr. did pretty well with Thoreau, Gandhi, and Reinhold Niebuhr as models—and remember, after all, whom King (and his father) were named for. The record hardly shows that "Eurocentric" education had such a terribly damaging effect on the psyche of great black Americans. Why deny it to black children today? Why not dwell with Du Bois above the veil? Is Lincoln to be a hero only for those

Born a slave in 1818, Frederick Douglass became the leading 19th-century spokesman for American blacks and devoted his life to the fight for black rights.

of English ancestry? Jackson only for Scotch-Irish? Douglass only for blacks? Great artists, thinkers, leaders are the possession not just of their own racial clan but of all humanity.

As for self-esteem, is this really the product of ethnic role models and fantasies of a glorious past? or does it not result from the belief in oneself that springs from achievement, from personal rather than from racial pride? Cohesive Asian-American and Jewish-American families instill in their children a sense of self-respect and a determination to work hard. For historical reasons, black families are often less cohesive, and in consequence many black kids often move into a mistrustful world with low self-worth and little self-confidence. Hearing about Africa won't change that.

VI

The use of history as therapy means the corruption of history as history. All major races, cultures, nations have committed crimes, atrocities, horrors at one time or another. Every civilization has skeletons in its closet. Honest history calls for the unexpurgated record. How much would a full account of African despotism, massacre, and slavery increase the self-esteem of black students? Yet what kind of history do you have if you leave out all the bad things?

Even if history is sanitized in order to make people feel good, there is no evidence that feel-good history promotes ethnic self-esteem and equips students to grapple with their lives. Afrocentric education, on the contrary, will make black children, as William Raspberry has written, "less competent in the culture in which they have to compete." After all, what good will it do young black Americans to take African names, wear African costumes, and replicate African rituals, to learn by music and mantras, rhythm and rapping, to reject standard English, to hear that because their minds work differently a first-class education is not for them? Will such training help them to understand democracy better? Help them to fit better into American life? "General Powell did not reach his present post," Jacques Barzun reminds us, "by believing that Black English was sufficient for the career he wanted to pursue."

Indeed, it is hard to imagine any form of education more likely than Afrocentrism to have a "terribly damaging effect on the psyche." The best way to keep a people down is to deny them the means of improvement and achievement and cut them off from the opportunities of the national life. If some Kleagle of the Ku Klux Klan wanted to devise an educational curriculum for the specific purpose of handicapping and disabling black Americans, he would not be likely to come up with anything more diabolically effective than Afrocentrism.

Moreover, will it increase their self-esteem when black children grow up and learn that many of the things the Afrocentrists taught them are not true? Black scholars have tried for years to rescue black history from chauvinistic hyperbole. A. A. Schomburg, the noted archivist of black history, expressed his scorn long ago for those who "glibly tried to prove that half of the world's geniuses have been Negroes and to trace the pedigree of nineteenth-century Americans from the Queen of Sheba."

The black sociologist Orlando Patterson writes with similar scorn of black educators who "head for the civilizational big-time: to Carthage and Egypt and Nubia and the rest of the 'great' civilizations of ancient North Africa. . . . The role of the Black historian is to get the Black man back into the wonderful 'birth of civilization' story, to prove that white history has been a big lie, that the Black man . . . was right there in all the major events of 'world history.'" Patterson calls it the three P's approach: black history as princes, pyramids, and pageantry.

The dean of black historians in America today is John Hope Franklin. "While a black scholar," Franklin writes, "has a clear responsibility to join in improving the society in which he lives, he must understand the difference between hard-hitting advocacy on the one hand and the highest standards of scholarship on the other." Serious black scholars like Henry Louis Gates of Duke regard Afrocentricity with skepticism. "I don't see any of those things as being peculiar to African-Americans. They sound like very vague attributes to me, and all kinds of cultures and societies have those same values. . . . I am certainly not in the same camp as Molefi Asante and all these guys."

Professor John Hope Franklin contends that black academics must understand the difference between racial advocacy and high standards of scholarship.

"These guys" are advocates not of cultural pluralism but of black ethnocentrism. Nor do they make much effort to disguise political motives. Asa Hilliard deals with scholarly critics not by responding to their criticisms but by calling any attack on the Afrocentric curriculum "an attack on the study of African people generally." Defending the New York task-force report, one of its authors called the proposed curricular revision "a powerful tool of cultural and political empowerment. I see a clear relationship in the effort to keep us weak and the recognition that we [the nonwhites] will be the majority in the 21st century."

Academia has its Al Sharptons too. It is notable how few respected black scholars attended Hilliard's 1990 convention, "The Infusion of African and African American Content in the School Curriculum." The excesses of Afrocentrism are now threatening to discredit the whole field of African-American studies.

VII

"Once ethnic pride and self-esteem become the criterion for teaching history," Diane Ravitch points out, "certain things cannot be taught." Skeletons must stay in the closet lest outing displease descendants.

No history curriculum in the country is more carefully wrought and better balanced in its cultural pluralism than California's. But hearings before the State Board of Education show what happens when ethnicity is unleashed at the expense of scholarship. At issue were textbooks responsive to the new curriculum. Polish-Americans demanded that any reference to Hitler's holocaust be accompanied by accounts of equivalent genocide suffered by Polish Christians. Armenian-Americans sought coverage of Turkish massacres; Turkish-Americans objected. Though black historians testified that the treatment of black history was exemplary, Afrocentrists said the schoolbooks would lead to "textbook genocide." Moslems complained that an illustration of an Islamic warrior with a raised scimitar stereotyped Moslems as "terrorists."

"One group after another," Ravitch recalls, "insisted that its forebears had suffered more than anyone else in history." American Indians, Hispanics, Chinese-Americans, homosexuals, born-again Christian fundamentalists, atheists—all protested that the schoolbooks had not gone far enough in celebrating their particular cultures or viewpoints. "The single theme that persistently ran through the hearings," Ravitch writes, "was that the critics did not want anything taught if it offended members of their group; whatever was taught, many claimed, must have a positive effect on the self-esteem or pride of their group. . . . The only villains in the history-for-self-esteem movement . . . are white males, who thus far have no spokesmen."

Professor Diane Ravitch asserts that "once ethnic pride and self-esteem become the criterion for teaching history, certain things cannot be taught."

In New York the curriculum guide for 11th-grade American history tells students that there were three "foundations" for the Constitution: the European Enlightenment, the "Haudenosaunee political system," and the antecedent colonial experience. Only the Haudenosaunee political system receives explanatory subheadings: "a. Influence upon colonial leadership and European intellectuals (Locke, Montesquieu, Voltaire, Rousseau); b. Impact on Albany Plan of Union, Articles of Confederation, and U. S. Constitution."

How many experts on the American Constitution would endorse this stirring tribute to the "Haudenosaunee political system"? How many have heard of that system? Whatever influence the Iroquois confederation may have had on the framers of the Constitution was marginal; on European intellectuals it was marginal to the point of invisibility. No other state curriculum offers this analysis of the making of the Constitution. But then no other state has so effective an Iroquois lobby.

The debate over the New York history curriculum produced thoughtful reactions from the state's history teachers. History, one wrote, "should not be a vehicle for pleasing or appeasing any social group, nor should teachers act as public-relations counselors for a cause. Writing history requires a critical analysis of a topic and not a laudatory exposition of its exploits." The Department of History at the State University of New York College at Brockport summed the question up in a circular letter to departments of history throughout the state: "We insist that the curriculum not be used as an instrument that is primarily designed to redress past injustices, however real. It is, rather, a tool with which to pursue the truths about our common past."

President Franklyn Jenifer of Howard University, while saying that "historical black institutions" like his own have a responsibility to teach young people about their particular history and culture, adds, "One has to be very careful when one is talking about public schools. . . . Public schools by their definition are schools that are open to all people, and should be cognizant of the needs of all of the people. . . . There should be no creation of nonexistent history."

When every ethnic and religious group claims a right to approve or veto anything that is taught in public schools, the fatal line is crossed between cultural pluralism and ethnocentrism. An evident casualty is the old idea that whatever our ethnic base, we are all Americans together.

Feel-good history, moreover, is a betrayal of a noble profession. "What I hate," Gore Vidal has well said, "is good citizenship history. That has wrecked every history book. Now we're getting, 'The Hispanics are warm and joyous and have brought such wonder into our lives,' you know, and before them the Jews, and before them the blacks. And the women. I mean, cut it out!"

Let us by all means teach black history, African history, women's history, Hispanic history, Asian history. But let us teach them as history, not as filiopietistic commemoration. The purpose of history is to promote not group self-esteem, but understanding of the world and the past, dispassionate analysis, judgment, and perspective, respect for divergent cultures and traditions, and unflinching protection for those unifying ideas of tolerance, democracy, and human rights that make free historical inquiry possible.

"I'm here to answer your questions around the clocks."

Mary Lucus-Fisher
Senior Customer Service Agent, Sacramento

Whatever you need to know—from prices, packaging tips and customs regulations
to the status of your shipment, pick-up to delivery—our Customer Service Centers can tell
you, quickly and courteously. Twenty-four hours a day.

CHAPTER 4

THE DECOMPOSITION OF AMERICA

Low self-esteem is too deep a malady to be cured by hearing nice things about one's own ethnic past. History is not likely to succeed where psychiatry fails. Afrocentrism in particular is an escape from the hard and expensive challenges of our society—the need for safer schools, better teachers, better teaching materials, greater investment in education; the need for stable families that can nourish self-discipline and aspiration; the need for jobs and income that can nourish stable families; the need to stop the ravages of drugs and crime; the need to overcome the racism still lurking in the interstices of American society. "The need," William Raspberry observes of his own people, "is not to reach back for some culture we never knew but to lay full claim to the culture in which we exist."

I

The ethnicity rage in general and Afrocentricity in particular not only divert attention from the real needs but exacerbate the problems. The recent apotheosis of ethnicity, black, brown, red, yellow, white, has revived the dismal prospect that in happy melting-pot days Americans thought the republic was moving safely beyond—that is, a society fragmented into ethnic groups. The cult of ethnicity exaggerates differences, intensifies resentments and antagonisms, drives ever deeper the awful wedges between races and nationalities. The endgame is self-pity and self-ghettoization.

Now there is a reasonable argument in the black case for a measure of regrouping and self-reliance as part of the preparation for entry into an integrated society on an equal basis. Integration on any other basis, it is contended, would mean total capitulation to white standards. Affirmation of racial and cultural pride is thus essential to true integration. One can see this as a psychological point, but as a cultural point?

For generations blacks have grown up in an American culture, on which they have had significant influence and to which they have made significant contributions. Self-Africanization after 300 years in America is playacting. Afrocentricity as expounded by ethnic ideologues implies Europhobia, separatism, emotions of alienation, victimization, paranoia. Most curious and unexpected of all is a black demand for the return of black-white segregation.

"To separate [black children] from others of similar age and qualifications solely because of their race," Chief Justice Warren wrote in the school-integration case, "generates a feeling of inferiority as to their status in the community that may affect their hearts and minds in a way unlikely ever to be undone." In 40 years doctrine has come full circle. Now integration is held to bring feelings of inferiority, and segregation to bring the cure.

This revival of separatism will begin, if the black educator Felix Boateng has his way, in the earliest grades. "The use of standard English as the only language of instruction," Boateng argues, "aggravates the process of deculturalization." A "culturally relevant curriculum" for minority children would recognize "the home and community dialect they bring to school." (Not all black educators, it should be said, share this desire to handicap black children from infancy. "One fact is clear," notes Janice Hale-Benson of Cleveland State University. "Speaking standard English is a skill needed by Black children for upward mobility in American society and it should be taught in early childhood.")

If any educational institution should bring people together as individuals in friendly and civil association, it should be the university. But the fragmentation of campuses in recent years into a multitude of ethnic organizations is spectacular—and disconcerting.

One finds black dormitories, black student unions, black fraternities and sororities, black business and law societies, black homosexual and lesbian groups, black tables in dining halls. Stanford, Dinesh D'Souza reports, has "ethnic theme houses." The University of Pennsylvania gives blacks—6 percent of the enrollment—their own yearbook. Campuses today, according to one University of Pennsylvania professor, have "the cultural diversity of Beirut. There are separate armed camps. The black kids don't mix with the white kids. The Asians are off by themselves. Oppression is the great status symbol."

Oberlin was for a century and half the model of a racially integrated college. "Increasingly," Jacob Weisberg, an editor at *The New Republic*, reports, "Oberlin students think, act, study, and live apart." Asians live in Asia House, Jews in "J" House, Latinos in Spanish House, blacks in African-Heritage House, foreign students in Third World House. Even the Lesbian, Gay, and Bisexual Union has broken up into racial and gender factions. "The result is separate worlds."

Huddling is an understandable reaction for any minority group faced with new and scary challenges. But institutionalized separatism only crystallizes racial differences and magnifies racial tensions. "Certain activities are labeled white and black," says a black student at Central Michigan University. "If you don't just participate in black activities, you are shunned." A recent study by the black anthropologist Signithia Fordham of Rutgers concludes that a big reason for black underachievement is the fear that academic success will be taken as a sellout to the white world. "What appears to have emerged in some segments of the black community," Fordham says, "is a kind of cultural orientation which defines academic learning in school as 'acting white.'"

Militants further argue that because only blacks can comprehend the black experience, only blacks should teach black history and literature, as, in the view of some feminists, only women should teach women's history and literature. "True diversity," according to the faculty's Budget Committee at the University of California at Berkeley, requires that courses match the ethnic and gender identities of the professors.

The doctrine that *only* blacks can teach and write black history leads inexorably to the doctrine that blacks can teach and write *only* black history as well as to inescapable corollaries: Chinese must be restricted to Chinese history, women to women's history, and so on. Henry Louis Gates criticizes "ghettoized programs where students and members of the faculty sit around and argue about whether a white person can think a black thought." As for the notion that there is a "mystique" about black studies that requires a person to have black skin in order to pursue them—that, John Hope Franklin observes succinctly, is "voodoo."

The voodoo principle is extended from scholarship to the arts. Thus the fine black playwright August Wilson insists on a black director for the film of his play *Fences*. "We have a different way of responding to the world," Wilson explains. "We have different ideas about religion, different manners of social intercourse. We have different ideas about style, about language. We have different esthetics [*sic*]. . . . The job requires someone who shares the specifics of the culture of black Americans. . . . Let's make a rule. Blacks don't direct Italian films. Italians don't direct Jewish films. Jews don't direct black American films." What a terrible rule that would be!

In the same restrictive spirit, Actors' Equity tried to prevent the British actor Jonathan Pryce from playing in New York the role he created in London in *Miss Saigon*, announcing that it could not condone "the casting of a Caucasian actor in the role of a Eurasian." (Pryce responded that, if this doctrine prevails, "I'd be stuck playing Welshmen for the rest of my life.") Equity did not, however, apply the same principle to the black actors Morgan Freeman and Denzel Washington who were both acting in Shakespeare at that time in New York. *The Wall Street Journal* acidly suggested that, according to the principle invoked, not only whites but the disabled should protest the casting of Denzel

The notion of racial separatism is reflected in August Wilson's insistence on a black director for the film of his play *Fences*.

Washington as Richard III because Washington lacked a hunchback.

The distinguished black social psychologist Kenneth B. Clark, whose findings influenced the Supreme Court's decision in the school-integration case, rejects the argument that blacks and whites must be separated "because they represent different cultures and that cultures, like oil and water, cannot mix." This, Clark says, is what white segregationists have argued for generations. He adds, "There is absolutely no evidence to support the contention that the inherent damage to human beings of primitive exclusion on the basis of race is any less damaging when demanded or enforced by the previous victims than when imposed by the dominant group."

II

The separatist impulse is by no means confined to the black community. Another salient expression is the bilingualism movement, ostensibly conducted in the interests of all non-English speakers but particularly a Hispanic-American project.

Bilingualism is hardly a new issue in American history. Seven years after the adoption of the Constitution, a proposal to print 3,000 sets of federal laws in German as well as English was narrowly defeated in the House of Representatives. (This incident gave rise to the myth, later cherished by Nazi propagandists like Colin Ross, that German had nearly displaced English as America's official language.) In the 19th century, newly arrived immigrants stayed for a season with their old language, used it in their homes, churches, newspapers, and not seldom in bilingual public schools, until acculturation reduced and the First World War discouraged the use of languages other than English.

In recent years the combination of the ethnicity cult with a flood of immigration from Spanish-speaking countries has given bilingualism new impetus. The presumed purpose is transitional: to move non-English-speaking children as quickly as possible from bilingual into all-English classes. The Bilingual Education Act of 1968 supplies guidelines and funding; the 1974 Supreme Court decision in *Lau* v. *Nichols* (a Chinese-speaking case) requires school districts to provide special programs for children who do not know English.

Alas, bilingualism has not worked out as planned: rather the contrary. Testimony is mixed, but indications are that bilingual education retards rather than expedites the movement of Hispanic children into the English-speaking world and that it promotes segregation more than it does integration. Bilingualism shuts doors. It nourishes self-ghettoization, and ghettoization nourishes racial antagonism. Bilingualism "encourages concentrations of Hispanics to stay together and not be integrated," says Alfredo Mathew Jr., a Hispanic civic leader, and it may well foster "a type of apartheid that will generate animosities with others, such as

Blacks, in the competition for scarce resources, and further alienate the Hispanic from the larger society."

Using some language other than English dooms people to second-class citizenship in American society. "Those who have the most to lose in a bilingual America," says the Mexican-American writer Richard Rodriguez, "are the foreign-speaking poor." Rodriguez recalls his own boyhood: "It would have pleased me to hear my teachers address me in Spanish. . . . But I would have delayed . . . having to learn the language of public society. . . . Only when I was able to think of myself as an American, no longer an alien in *gringo* society, could I seek the rights and opportunities necessary for full public individuality."

Monolingual education opens doors to the larger world. "I didn't speak English until I was about 8 years of age," Governor Mario Cuomo recently recalled, "and there was a kind of traumatic entry into public school. It made an immense impression on me." Traumatic or not, public school taught Cuomo the most effective English among politicos of his generation.

Yet a professor at the University of Massachusetts told Rosalie Pedalino Porter, whose long experience in bilingual education led to her excellent book *Forked Tongue*, that teaching English to children reared in another language is a form of political oppression. Her rejoinder seems admirable: "When we succeed in helping our students use the majority language fluently . . . we are empowering our students rather than depriving them."

Mexican-American author Richard Rodriguez deplores bilingualism, saying that the people who have the most to lose in America are the foreign-speaking poor.

Panicky conservatives, fearful that the republic is over the hill, call for a constitutional amendment to make English the official language of the United States. Seventeen states already have such statutes. This is a poor idea. The English language does not need statutory reinforcement and the drive for an amendment will only increase racial discrimination and resentment.

Nonetheless, a common language is a necessary bond of national cohesion in so heterogeneous a nation as America. The bilingual campaign has created both an educational establishment with a vested interest in extending the bilingual empire and a political lobby with a vested interest in retaining a Hispanic constituency. Like Afrocentricity and the ethnicity cult, bilingualism is an elitist, not a popular, movement—"romantic ethnicity," as Myrdal called it; political ethnicity too. Still, institutionalized bilingualism remains another source of the fragmentation of America, another threat to the dream of "one people."

III

Most ominous about the separatist impulses is the meanness generated when one group is set against another. What Harold Isaacs, that acute student of racial sensitivities and resentments, called the "built-in we-they syndrome" has caused more dominating, fearing, hating, killing than any other single cause since time began.

Blacks, having suffered most grievously (at least in America) from persecution, have perhaps the greatest susceptibility to paranoia—remembering always that even paranoids may have real enemies. After all, considering what we now know about the plots against black Americans concocted by J. Edgar Hoover and executed by his FBI, who can blame blacks for being forever suspicious of white intentions?

Still, the *New York Times*-WCBS-TV poll of New Yorkers in 1990 is startling. Sixty percent of black respondents thought it true or possibly true that the government was making drugs available in black neighborhoods in order to harm black people. Twenty-nine percent thought it true or possibly true that the AIDS virus was invented by racist conspirators to kill blacks.

The irrepressible Leonard Jeffries of CCNY observed that "AIDS coming out of a laboratory and finding itself localized in certain populations certainly has to be looked at as part of a conspiratorial process." After a Jeffries class, 10 black students told the *Times* reporter that AIDS and drugs were indeed part of a white conspiracy. "During the Carter administration," one said, "there was a document put out that said by the year 2000, one hundred billion Africans had to be destroyed." "Because of who's being devastated the most, and growing up in the U.S. and knowing the history of slavery and racism in this country," an older black man said, "you can't be black and not feel that AIDS is some kind of experiment, some kind of plot to hit undesirable minority populations."

Nor is such speculation confined to the feverish sidewalks of New York. "Let me make a speech before a black audience," testifies William Raspberry, "and sometime during the Q & A someone is certain to ask if I believe there is a conspiracy against black Americans. It doesn't matter whether the subject is drugs or joblessness, school failure or teen pregnancy, politics or immigration. I can count on hearing some version of the conspiracy question."

The black case is only a more extreme version of the persecution complex—the feeling that someone is out to get them—to which nearly all minorities on occasion succumb. Mutual suspicion and hostility are bound to emerge in a society bent on defining itself in terms of jostling and competing groups.

IV

"The era that began with the dream of integration," Richard Rodriguez has observed, "ended up with scorn for assimilation." Instead of casting off the foreign skin, as John Quincy Adams had stipulated, never to resume it, the fashion is to resume the foreign skin as conspicuously as can be. The cult of ethnicity has reversed the movement of American history, producing a nation of minorities—or at least of minority spokesmen—less interested in joining with the majority in common endeavor than in declaring their alienation from an oppressive, white, patriarchal, racist, sexist, classist society. The ethnic ideology inculcates the illusion that membership in one or another ethnic group is the basic American experience.

Most Americans, it is true, continue to see themselves primarily as individuals and only secondarily and trivially as adherents of a group. Nor is harm done when ethnic groups display pride in their historic past or in their contributions to the American present. But the division of society into fixed ethnicities nourishes a culture of victimization and a contagion of inflammable sensitivities. And when a vocal and visible minority pledges primary allegiance to their groups, whether ethnic, sexual, religious, or, in rare cases (communist, fascist), political, it presents a threat to the brittle bonds of national identity that hold this diverse and fractious society together.

A peculiarly ugly mood seems to have settled over the one arena where freedom of inquiry and expression should be most unconstrained and civility most respected—our colleges and universities. It is no fun running a university these days. Undergraduates can be wanton and cruel in their exclusion, their harassment, their heavy pranks, their wounding invective. Minority students, for the most understandable reasons, are often vulnerable and frightened. Racial cracks, slurs, insults, vilification pose difficult problems. Thus posters appear around the campus at the University of Michigan parodying the slogan of the United Negro College Fund: A MIND IS A TERRIBLE THING TO WASTE—ESPECIALLY ON A NIGGER. Decent white students join the protest against white bullies and thugs.

Presidents and deans begin to ask themselves, which is more important—protecting free speech or preventing racial persecution? The Constitution, Justice Holmes said, embodies "the principle of free thought—not free thought for those who agree with us but freedom for the thought that we hate." But suppose the thought we hate undercuts the Constitution's ideal of equal justice under law? Does not the First Amendment protect equality as well as liberty? how to draw a bright line between speech and behavior?

One has a certain sympathy for besieged administrators who, trying to do their best to help minority students, adopt regulations to restrict racist and sexist speech. More than a hundred institutions, according to the American Civil Liberties Union, had done so by February 1991. My own decided preference is to stand by the First Amendment and to fight speech by speech, not by censorship. But then, I am not there on the firing line.

One can even understand why administrators, not sure what best to do for minorities and eager to keep things quiet, accept—even subsidize—separatist remedies urged by student militants. They might, however, ponder Kenneth Clark's comment: "The white liberal . . . who concedes black separatism so hastily and benevolently must look to his own reasons, not the least of them perhaps an exquisite relief." And it is sad, though instructive, that the administrations especially disposed to encourage racial and ethnic enclaves—like Berkeley, Michigan, Oberlin, the University of Massachusetts at Amherst—are, Dinesh D'Souza (himself an Indian from India) points out, the ones experiencing the most racial tension. Troy Duster, a Berkeley sociologist, finds a correlation between group separatism and racial hostility among students.

Moderates who would prefer fending for themselves as individuals are bullied into going along with their group. Groups get committed to platforms and to we-they syndromes. Faculty members appease. A code of ideological orthodoxy emerges. The code's guiding principle is that nothing should be said that might give offense to members of minority groups (and, apparently, that anything can be said that gives offense to white males of European origin).

The Office of Student Affairs at Smith College has put out a bulletin listing types of oppression for people belatedly "realizing that they are oppressed." Some samples of the Smith litany of sins:

Dinesh D'Souza, author of the recently published book Illiberal Education, writes that American students are being educated "in close-mindedness and intolerance."

> ABLEISM: Oppression of the differently abled by the temporarily able.
>
> HETEROSEXISM: Oppression of those of sexual orientation other than heterosexual, such as gays, lesbians, and bisexuals; this can take place by not acknowledging their existence.
>
> LOOKISM: The belief that appearance is an indicator of a person's value; the construction of a standard for beauty/attractiveness; and oppression through stereotypes and generalizations of both those who do not fit that standard and those who do.

Can they be kidding up there in Northampton?

The code imposes standards of what is called, now rather derisively, "political correctness." What began as a means of controlling student incivility threatens to become, formally or informally, a means of controlling curricula and faculty too. Clark University asks professors proposing courses to explain how "pluralistic (minority, women, etc.) views and concerns are explored and integrated in this course." A philosopher declined to sign, doubting that the university would ask professors to explain how "patriotic and pro-family values are explored and integrated."

Two distinguished American historians at Harvard, Bernard Bailyn and Stephan Thernstrom, offered a course in population history called

"The Peopling of America." Articles appeared in the *Harvard Crimson* criticizing the professors for "racial insensitivity," and black students eventually presented them with a bill of particulars. Thernstrom, an advocate of ethnic history, the editor of the *Harvard Encyclopedia of American Ethnic Groups*, was accused of racism. He had, it developed, used the term "Indians" instead of "Native Americans." He had also referred to "Oriental" religion—the adjective was deemed "colonial and imperialistic." Bailyn had recommended diaries of Southern planters without recommending slave narratives. And so on, for six single-spaced pages.

The episode reminds one of the right-wing students who in Joe McCarthy days used to haunt the classrooms of liberal Harvard professors (like me) hoping to catch whiffs of Marxism emanating from the podium. Thernstrom decided to hell with it and gave up the course. A signal triumph for political correctness.

Academic radicals pay little attention to talk about academic freedom or scholarly standards. "Under the guise of defending objectivity and intellectual rigor, which is a lot of mishmash," says Catharine Stimpson, dean of the graduate school at Rutgers, "they are trying to preserve the cultural and political supremacy of white heterosexual males."

Those who stand up for what they believe invite smear campaigns. A favorite target these days is Diane Ravitch of Columbia's Teachers College, a first-class historian of American education, an enlightened advocate of school reform, and a steadfast champion of cultural pluralism. She is dedicated to reasoned and temperate argument and is perseveringly conciliatory rather than polemical in her approach. Perhaps the fact that she is a woman persuades ethnic chauvinists that they can bully her. Despite nasty efforts at intimidation, she continues to expose the perils of ethnocentrism with calm lucidity.

Ravitch's unpardonable offense seems to be her concern about *unum* as well as about *pluribus*—her belief that history should help us understand how bonds of cohesion make us a nation rather than an irascible collection of unaffiliated groups. For in the end, the cult of ethnicity defines the republic not as a polity of individuals but as a congeries of distinct and inviolable cultures. When a student sent a memorandum to the "diversity education committee" at the University of Pennsylvania mentioning her "deep regard for the individual," a college administrator returned the paper with the word *individual* underlined: "This is a *red flag* phrase today, which is considered by many to be *racist*. Arguments that champion the individual over the group ultimately privileges [*sic*] the 'individuals' belonging to the largest or dominant group."

The contemporary sanctification of the group puts the old idea of a coherent society at stake. Multicultural zealots reject as hegemonic the notion of a shared commitment to common ideals. How far the discourse has come from Crèvecoeur's "new race," from Tocqueville's civic participation, from Emerson's "smelting pot," from Bryce's "amazing solvent," from Myrdal's "American Creed"!

Yet what has held the American people together in the absence of a common ethnic origin has been precisely a common adherence to ideals of democracy and human rights that, too often transgressed in practice, forever goad us to narrow the gap between practice and principle.

The American synthesis has an inevitable Anglo-Saxon coloration, but it is no longer an exercise in Anglo-Saxon domination. The republic embodies ideals that transcend ethnic, religious, and political lines. It is an experiment, reasonably successful for a while, in creating a common identity for people of diverse races, religions, languages, cultures. But the experiment can continue to succeed only so long as Americans continue to believe in the goal. If the republic now turns away from Washington's old goal of "one people," what is its future?—disintegration of the national community, apartheid, Balkanization, tribalization?

"The one absolutely certain way of bringing this nation to ruin, of preventing all possibility of its continuing to be a nation at all," said Theodore Roosevelt, "would be to permit it to become a tangle of squabbling nationalities, an intricate knot of German-Americans, Irish-Americans, English-Americans, French-Americans, Scandinavian-Americans, or Italian-Americans, each preserving its separate nationality." Three-quarters of a century later we must add a few more nationalities to T. R.'s brew. This only strengthens his point.

BLK

"You're looking at one of our biggest priorities."

Dean Martin
Ramp Agent, Newark

At Federal Express, we don't just deliver documents and small packages throughout the world. We also deliver big packages, big crates, and big containers throughout the world. In a big hurry.

CHAPTER
5

E PLURIBUS UNUM?

The attack on the common American identity is the culmination of the cult of ethnicity. That attack was mounted in the first instance by European Americans of non-British origin ("unmeltable ethnics") against the British foundations of American culture; then, latterly and massively, by Americans of non-European origin against the European foundations of that culture. As Theodore Roosevelt's foreboding suggests, the European immigration itself palpitated with internal hostilities, everyone at everybody else's throats—hardly the "monocultural" crowd portrayed by ethnocentric separatists. After all, the two great "world" wars of the 20th century began as fights among European states. Making a single society out of this diversity of antagonistic European peoples is a hard enough job. The new salience of non-European, nonwhite stocks compounds the challenge. And the non-Europeans, or at least their self-appointed spokesmen, bring with them a resentment, in some cases a hatred, of Europe and the West provoked by generations of Western colonialism, racism, condescension, contempt, and cruel exploitation.

I

Will not this rising flow of non-European immigrants create a "minority majority" that will make Eurocentrism obsolete by the 21st century? This is the fear of some white Americans and the hope (and sometimes the threat) of some nonwhites.

Immigrants were responsible for a third of population growth during the 1980s. More arrived than in any decade since the second of the century. And the composition of the newcomers changed dramatically. In 1910 nearly 90 percent of immigrants came from Europe. In the 1980s more than 80 percent came from Asia and Latin America.

Still, foreign-born residents constitute only about 7 percent of the population today as against nearly 15 percent when the first Roosevelt and Wilson were worrying about hyphenated Americans. Stephan

Thernstrom doubts that the minority majority will ever arrive. The black share in the population has grown rather slowly—9.9 percent in 1920, 10 percent in 1950, 11.1 percent in 1970, 12.1 percent in 1990. Neither Asian-Americans nor Hispanic-Americans go in for especially large families; and family size in any case tends to decline as income and intermarriage increase. "If today's immigrants assimilate to American ways as readily as their predecessors at the turn of the century—as seems to be happening," Thernstrom concludes, "there won't be a minority majority issue anyway."

America has so long seen itself as the asylum for the oppressed and persecuted—and has done itself and the world so much good thereby—that any curtailment of immigration offends something in the American soul. No one wants to be a Know-Nothing. Yet uncontrolled immigration is an impossibility; so the criteria of control are questions the American democracy must confront. We have shifted the basis of admission three times this century—from national origins in 1924 to family reunification in 1965 to needed skills in 1990. The future of immigration policy depends on the capacity of the assimilation process to continue to do what it has done so well in the past: to lead newcomers to an acceptance of the language, the institutions, and the political ideals that hold the nation together.

II

Is Europe really the root of all evil? The crimes of Europe against lesser breeds without the law (not to mention even worse crimes—Hitlerism and Stalinism—against other Europeans) are famous. But these crimes do not alter other facts of history: that Europe was the birthplace of the United States of America, that European ideas and culture formed the republic, that the United States is an extension of European civilization, and that nearly 80 percent of Americans are of European descent.

When Irving Howe, hardly a notorious conservative, dared write, "The Bible, Homer, Plato, Sophocles, Shakespeare are central to our culture," an outraged reader ("having graduated this past year from Amherst") wrote, "Where on Howe's list is the *Quran*, the *Gita*, Confucius, and other central cultural artifacts of the peoples of our nation?" No one can doubt the importance of these works nor the influence they have had on other societies. But on American society? It may be too bad that dead white European males have played so large a role in shaping our culture. But that's the way it is. One cannot erase history.

These humdrum historical facts, and not some dastardly imperialist conspiracy, explain the Eurocentric slant in American schools. Would anyone seriously argue that teachers should conceal the European origins of American civilization? or that schools should educate the 20 percent and ignore the 80 percent? Of course the 20 percent and their contributions should be integrated into the curriculum too, which is the point of cultural pluralism.

But self-styled "multiculturalists" are very often ethnocentric separatists who see little in the Western heritage beyond Western crimes. The Western tradition, in this view, is inherently racist, sexist, "classist," hegemonic; irredeemably repressive, irredeemably oppressive. The spread of Western culture is due not to any innate quality but simply to the spread of Western power. Thus the popularity of European classical music around the world—and, one supposes, of American jazz and rock too—is evidence not of wide appeal but of "the pattern of imperialism, in which the conquered culture adopts that of the conqueror."

Such animus toward Europe lay behind the well-known crusade against the Western-civilization course at Stanford ("Hey-hey, ho-ho, Western culture's got to go!"). According to the National Endowment for the Humanities, students can graduate from 78 percent of American colleges and universities without taking a course in the history of Western civilization. A number of institutions—among them Dartmouth, Wisconsin, Mt. Holyoke—require courses in third-world or ethnic studies but not in Western civilization. The mood is one of divesting Americans of the sinful European inheritance and seeking redemptive infusions from non-Western cultures.

III

One of the oddities of the situation is that the assault on the Western tradition is conducted very largely with analytical weapons forged in the West. What are the names invoked by the coalition of latter-day Marxists, deconstructionists, poststructuralists, radical feminists, Afrocentrists? Marx, Nietzsche, Gramsci, Derrida, Foucault, Lacan, Sartre, de Beauvoir, Habermas, the Frankfurt "critical theory" school—Europeans all. The "unmasking," "demythologizing," "decanonizing," "dehegomizing" blitz against Western culture depends on methods of critical analysis unique to the West—which surely testifies to the internally redemptive potentialities of the Western tradition.

Even Afrocentrists seem to accept subliminally the very Eurocentric standards they think they are rejecting. "Black intellectuals condemn Western civilization," Professor Pearce Williams says, "yet ardently wish to prove it was founded by their ancestors." And, like Frantz Fanon and Léopold Senghor, whose books figure prominently on their reading lists, Afrocentric ideologues are intellectual children of the West they repudiate. Fanon, the eloquent spokesman of the African wretched of the earth, had French as his native tongue and based his analyses on Freud, Marx, and Sartre. Senghor, the prophet of Negritude, wrote in French, established the Senegalese educational system on the French model and, when he left the presidency of Senegal, retired to France.

Western hegemony, it would seem, can be the source of protest as well as of power. Indeed, the invasion of American schools by the Afrocentric curriculum, not to mention the conquest of university departments of English and comparative literature by deconstructionists, poststructuralists, etc., are developments that by themselves refute the extreme theory of "cultural hegemony." Of course, Gramsci had a point. Ruling values do dominate and permeate any society; but they do not have the rigid and monolithic grip on American democracy that academic leftists claim.

Radical academics denounce the "canon" as an instrument of European oppression enforcing the hegemony of the white race, the male sex, and the capitalist class, designed, in the words of one professor, "to rewrite the past and construct the present from the perspective of the privileged and the powerful." Or in the elegant words of another—and a professor of theological ethics at that: "The canon of great literature was created by high Anglican assholes to underwrite their social class."

The poor old canon is seen not only as conspiratorial but as static. Yet nothing changes more regularly and reliably than the canon: compare, for example, the canon in American poetry as defined by Edmund Clarence Stedman in his *Poets of America* (1885) with the canon of 1935 or of 1985 (whatever happened to Longfellow and Whittier?); or recall the changes that have overtaken the canonical literature of American history in the last half-century (who reads Beard and Parrington now?). And the critics clearly have no principled objection to the idea of the canon. They simply wish to replace an old gang by a new gang. After all, a canon means only that because you can't read everything, you give some books priority over others.

Oddly enough, serious Marxists—Marx and Engels, Lukacs, Trotsky, Gramsci—had the greatest respect for what Lukacs called "the classical heritage of mankind." Well they should have, for most great literature and much good history are deeply subversive in their impact on orthodoxies. Consider the present-day American literary canon: Emerson, Jefferson, Melville, Whitman, Hawthorne, Thoreau, Lincoln, Twain, Dickinson, William and Henry James, Henry Adams, Holmes, Dreiser, Faulkner, O'Neill. Lackeys of the ruling class? Apologists for the privileged and the powerful? Agents of American imperialism? Come on!

It is time to adjourn the chat about hegemony. If hegemony were as real as the cultural radicals pretend, Afrocentrism would never have got anywhere, and the heirs of William Lyon Phelps would still be running the Modern Language Association.

IV

Is the Western tradition a bar to progress and a curse on humanity? Would it really do America and the world good to get rid of the European legacy?

"あなたの街をとても良く知っている
フェデラル・エクスプレスです。"

Jun Funabashi
Courier, Tokyo

"When it comes to the international shipping business,
we know our way around like the natives. Because we *are* the natives."

No doubt Europe has done terrible things, not least to itself. But what culture has not? History, said Edward Gibbon, is little more than the register of the crimes, follies, and misfortunes of mankind. The sins of the West are no worse than the sins of Asia or of the Middle East or of Africa.

There remains, however, a crucial difference between the Western tradition and the others. The crimes of the West have produced their own antidotes. They have provoked great movements to end slavery, to raise the status of women, to abolish torture, to combat racism, to defend freedom of inquiry and expression, to advance personal liberty and human rights.

Whatever the particular crimes of Europe, that continent is also the source—the *unique* source—of those liberating ideas of individual liberty, political democracy, the rule of law, human rights, and cultural freedom that constitute our most precious legacy and to which most of the world today aspires. These are *European* ideas, not Asian, nor African, nor Middle Eastern ideas, except by adoption.

The freedoms of inquiry and of artistic creation, for example, are Western values. Consider the differing reactions to the case of Salman Rushdie: what the West saw as an intolerable attack on individual freedom the Middle East saw as a proper punishment for an evildoer who had violated the mores of his group. Individualism itself is looked on with abhorrence and dread by collectivist cultures in which loyalty to the group overrides personal goals—cultures that, social scientists say, comprise about 70 percent of the world's population.

There is surely no reason for Western civilization to have guilt trips laid on it by champions of cultures based on despotism, superstition, tribalism, and fanaticism. In this regard the Afrocentrists are especially absurd. The West needs no lectures on the superior virtue of those "sun people" who sustained slavery until Western imperialism abolished it (and, it is reported, sustain it to this day in Mauritania and the Sudan), who still keep women in subjection and cut off their clitorises, who carry out racial persecutions not only against Indians and other Asians but against fellow Africans from the wrong tribes, who show themselves either incapable of operating a democracy or ideologically hostile to the democratic idea, and who in their tyrannies and massacres, their Idi Amins and Boukassas, have stamped with utmost brutality on human rights.

Certainly the European overlords did little enough to prepare Africa for self-government. But democracy would find it hard in any case to put down roots in a tribalist and patrimonial culture that, long before the West invaded Africa, had sacralized the personal authority of chieftains and ordained the submission of the rest. What the West would call corruption is regarded through much of Africa as no more than the

The Statue of Liberty, symbolizing democracy and freedom, seemed to mean more to students and other demonstrators who mobbed Tiananmen Square in the spring of 1989 than it does to Americans.

prerogative of power. Competitive political parties, an independent judiciary, a free press, the rule of law are alien to African traditions.

It was the French, not the Algerians, who freed Algerian women from the veil (much to the irritation of Frantz Fanon, who regarded de-veiling as symbolic rape); as in India it was the British, not the Indians, who ended (or did their best to end) the horrible custom of *suttee*—widows burning themselves alive on their husbands' funeral pyres. And it was the West, not the non-Western cultures, that launched the crusade to abolish slavery—and in doing so encountered mighty resistance, especially in the Islamic world (where Moslems, with fine impartiality, enslaved whites as well as blacks). Those many brave and humane Africans who are struggling these days for decent societies are animated by Western, not by African, ideals. White guilt can be pushed too far.

The Western commitment to human rights has unquestionably been intermittent and imperfect. Yet the ideal remains—and movement toward it has been real, if sporadic. Today it is the *Western* democratic tradition that attracts and empowers people of all continents, creeds, and colors. When the Chinese students cried and died for democracy in Tiananmen Square, they brought with them not representations of Confucius or Buddha but a model of the Statue of Liberty.

V

The great American asylum, as Crèvecoeur called it, open, as Washington said, to the oppressed and persecuted of all nations, has been from the start an experiment in a multi-ethnic society. This is a bolder experiment than we sometimes remember. History is littered with the wreck of states that tried to combine diverse ethnic or linguistic or religious groups within a single sovereignty. Today's headlines tell of imminent crisis or impending dissolution in one or another multi-ethnic polity—the Soviet Union, India, Yugoslavia, Czechoslovakia, Ireland, Belgium, Canada, Lebanon, Cyprus, Israel, Ceylon, Spain, Nigeria, Kenya, Angola, Trinidad, Guyana. . . . The list is almost endless. The luck so far of the American experiment has been due in large part to the vision of the melting pot. "No other nation," Margaret Thatcher has said, "has so successfully combined people of different races and nations within a single culture."

But even in the United States, ethnic ideologues have not been without effect. They have set themselves against the old American ideal of assimilation. They call on the republic to think in terms not of individual but of group identity and to move the polity from individual rights to group rights. They have made a certain progress in transforming the United States into a more segregated society. They have done their best to turn a college generation against Europe and the Western tradition. They have imposed ethnocentric, Afrocentric, and bilingual curricula on public schools, well designed to hold minority children out of American society. They have told young people from minority groups that the Western democratic tradition is not for them. They have encouraged minorities to see themselves as victims and to live by alibis rather than to claim the opportunities opened for them by the potent combination of black protest and white guilt. They have filled the air with recrimination and rancor and have remarkably advanced the fragmentation of American life.

Yet I believe the campaign against the idea of common ideals and a single society will fail. Gunnar Myrdal was surely right: for all the damage it has done, the upsurge of ethnicity is a superficial enthusiasm stirred by romantic ideologues and unscrupulous hucksters whose claim to speak for their minorities is thoughtlessly accepted by the media. I doubt that the ethnic vogue expresses a reversal of direction from assimilation to apartheid among the minorities themselves. Indeed, the more the ideologues press the case for ethnic separatism, the less they appeal to the mass of their own groups. They have thus far done better in intimidating the white majority than in converting their own constituencies.

"No nation in history," writes Lawrence Fuchs, the political scientist and immigration expert in his fine book *The American Kaleidoscope*, "had proved as successful as the United States in managing ethnic diversity. No nation before had ever made diversity itself a source of national identity and unity." The second sentence explains the success described in the first, and the mechanism for translating diversity into unity has been the American Creed, the civic culture—the very assimilating, unifying culture that is today challenged, and not seldom rejected, by the ideologues of ethnicity.

A historian's guess is that the resources of the Creed have not been exhausted. Americanization has not lost its charms. Many sons and daughters of ethnic neighborhoods still want to shed their ethnicity and move to the suburbs as fast as they can—where they will be received with far more tolerance than they would have been 70 years ago. The desire for achievement and success in American society remains a potent force for assimilation. Ethnic subcultures, Stephen Steinberg, author of *The Ethnic Myth*, points out, fade away "because circumstances forced them to make choices that undermined the basis for cultural survival."

Others may enjoy their ethnic neighborhoods but see no conflict between foreign descent and American loyalty. Unlike the multi-culturalists, they celebrate not only what is distinctive in their own backgrounds but what they hold in common with the rest of the population.

The ethnic identification often tends toward superficiality. The sociologist Richard Alba's study of children and grandchildren of immigrants in the Albany, New York, area shows the most popular "ethnic experience" to be sampling the ancestral cuisine. Still, less than half the respondents picked that, and only 1 percent ate ethnic food every day. Only one-fifth acknowledged a sense of special relationship to people of their own ethnic background; less than one-sixth taught their children about their ethnic origins; almost none was fluent in the language of the old country. "It is hard to avoid the conclusion," Alba writes, "that ethnic experience is shallow for the great majority of whites."

If ethnic experience is a good deal less shallow for blacks, it is because of their bitter experience in America, not because of their memories of Africa. Nonetheless most blacks prefer "black" to "African-Americans," fight bravely and patriotically for their country, and would move to the suburbs too if income and racism would permit.

As for Hispanic-Americans, first-generation Hispanics born in the United States speak English fluently, according to a Rand Corporation study; more than half of second-generation Hispanics give up Spanish altogether. When *Vista*, an English-language monthly for Hispanics, asked its readers what historical figures they most admired, Washington, Lincoln, and Theodore Roosevelt led the list, with Benito Juárez trailing behind as fourth, and Eleanor Roosevelt and Martin Luther King Jr. tied for fifth. So much for ethnic role models.

Nor, despite the effort of ethnic ideologues, are minority groups all that hermetically sealed off from each other, except in special situations, like colleges, where ideologues are authority figures. The wedding notices in any newspaper testify to the increased equanimity with which people these days marry across ethnic lines, across religious lines, even, though to a smaller degree, across racial lines. Around half of Asian-American marriages are with non-Orientals, and the Census Bureau estimates one million interracial—mostly black-white—marriages in 1990 as against 310,000 in 1970.

VI

The ethnic revolt against the melting pot has reached the point, in rhetoric at least, though not I think in reality, of a denial of the idea of a common culture and a single society. If large numbers of people really accept this, the republic would be in serious trouble. The question poses itself: how to restore the balance between *unum* and *pluribus*?

The old American homogeneity disappeared well over a century ago, never to return. Ever since, we have been preoccupied in one way or another with the problem, as Herbert Croly phrased it 80 years back in *The Promise of American Life*, "of preventing such divisions from dissolving the society into which they enter—of keeping such a highly differentiated society fundamentally sound and whole." This required, Croly believed, an "ultimate bond of union." There was only one way by which solidarity could be restored, "and that is by means of a democratic social ideal . . . "

The genius of America lies in its capacity to forge a single nation from peoples of remarkably diverse racial, religious, and ethnic origins. It has done so because democratic principles provide both the philosophical bond of union and practical experience in civic participation. The American Creed envisages a nation composed of individuals making their own choices and accountable to themselves, not a nation based on inviolable ethnic communities. The Constitution turns on individual rights, not on group rights. Law, in order to rectify past wrongs, has from time to time (and in my view often properly so) acknowledged the claims of groups; but this is the exception, not the rule.

Our democratic principles contemplate an open society founded on tolerance of differences and on mutual respect. In practice, America has been more open to some than to others. But it is more open to all today than it was yesterday and is likely to be even more open tomorrow than today. The steady movement of American life has been from exclusion to inclusion.

Historically and culturally this republic has an Anglo-Saxon base; but from the start the base has been modified, enriched, and reconstituted by transfusions from other continents and civilizations. The movement from exclusion to inclusion causes a constant revision in the texture of our culture. The ethnic transfusions affect all aspects of American life— our politics, our literature, our music, our painting, our movies, our cuisine, our customs, our dreams.

Black Americans in particular have influenced the ever-changing national culture in many ways. They have lived here for centuries, and, unless one believes in racist mysticism, they belong far more to American culture than to the culture of Africa. Their history is part of the Western democratic tradition, not an alternative to it. No one does black Americans more disservice than those Afrocentric ideologues who would define them out of the West.

The interplay of diverse traditions produces the America we know. "Paradoxical though it may seem," Diane Ravitch has well said, "the United States has a common culture that is multicultural." That is why unifying political ideals coexist so easily and cheerfully with diversity in social and cultural values. Within the overarching political commitment, people are free to live as they choose, ethnically and otherwise. Differences will remain; some are reinvented; some are used to drive us apart. But as we renew our allegiance to the unifying ideals, we provide the solvent that will prevent differences from escalating into antagonism and hatred.

One powerful reason for the movement from exclusion to inclusion is that the American Creed facilitates the appeal from the actual to the ideal. When we talk of the American democratic faith, we must understand it in its true dimensions. It is not an impervious, final, and complacent orthodoxy, intolerant of deviation and dissent, fulfilled in flag salutes, oaths of allegiance, and hands over the heart. It is an ever-evolving philosophy, fulfilling its ideals through debate, self-criticism, protest, disrespect, and irreverence; a tradition in which all have rights of heterodoxy and opportunities for self-assertion. The Creed has been the means by which Americans have haltingly but persistently narrowed the gap between performance and principle. It is what all Americans should learn, because it is what binds all Americans together.

Let us by all means in this increasingly mixed-up world learn about those other continents and civilizations. But let us master our own history first. Lamentable as some may think it, we inherit an American experience, as America inherits a European experience. To deny the essentially European origins of American culture is to falsify history.

Americans of whatever origin should take pride in the distinctive inheritance to which they have all contributed, as other nations take pride in their distinctive inheritances. Belief in one's own culture does not require disdain for other cultures. But one step at a time: no culture can hope to ingest other cultures all at once, certainly not before it ingests its own. As we begin to master our own culture, then we can explore the world.

Our schools and colleges have a responsibility to teach history for its own sake—as part of the intellectual equipment of civilized persons—and not to degrade history by allowing its contents to be dictated by pressure groups, whether political, economic, religious, or ethnic. The past may sometimes give offense to one or another minority; that is no reason for rewriting history. Giving pressure groups vetoes over text-books and courses betrays both history and education. Properly taught, history will convey a sense of the variety, continuity, and adaptability of cultures, of the need for understanding other cultures, of the ability of individuals and peoples to overcome obstacles, of the importance of critical analysis and dispassionate judgment in every area of life.

Above all, history can give a sense of national identity. We don't have to believe that our values are absolutely better than the next fellow's or the next country's, but we have no doubt that they are better *for us*, reared as we are—and are worth living by and worth dying for. For our values are not matters of whim and happenstance. History has given them to us. They are anchored in our national experience, in our great national documents, in our national heroes, in our folkways, traditions, and standards. People with a different history will have differing values. But we believe that our own are better for us. They work for us; and, for that reason, we live and die by them.

It has taken time to make the values real for all our citizens, and we still have a good distance to go, but we have made progress. If we now repudiate the quite marvelous inheritance that history bestows on us, we invite the fragmentation of the national community into a quarrelsome spatter of enclaves, ghettos, tribes. The bonds of cohesion in our society are sufficiently fragile, or so it seems to me, that it makes no sense to strain them by encouraging and exalting cultural and linguistic apartheid.

The American identity will never be fixed and final; it will always be in the making. Changes in the population have always brought changes in the national ethos and will continue to do so; but not, one must hope, at the expense of national integration. The question America confronts as a pluralistic society is how to vindicate cherished cultures and traditions without breaking the bonds of cohesion—common ideals, common political institutions, common language, common culture, common fate—that hold the republic together.

Our task is to combine due appreciation of the splendid diversity of the nation with due emphasis on the great unifying Western ideas of individual freedom, political democracy, and human rights. These are the ideas that define the American nationality—and that today empower people of all continents, races, and creeds.

"What then is the American, this new man? . . . Here individuals of all nations are melted into a new race of men." Still a good answer—still the best hope.

"We didn't just start an air express service. We started a revolution."

At Federal Express, we do a lot more than deliver packages and freight swiftly and dependably to more than 120 countries worldwide. We work in partnership with companies to design and operate the most sophisticated business logistics systems in the world. This allows companies to expand their markets, improve productivity, and compete more efficiently in a rapidly-changing global economy. You could call it revolutionary.

NOTES ON SOURCES

FOREWORD
■ The quotation on p. 1 is from Letter III in Crève-coeur's *Letters From an American Farmer* (1782). Emphasis added.

CHAPTER 1
■ The first quotation on p. 6 is from Thomas Paine's *Common Sense*, appendix; the second is from Herman Melville's *White Jacket*, chap. 36; the third is from Melville's *Redburn*, chap. 33.
■ Emerson's quotation on p. 6 is from *Emerson in His Journals*, ed. Joel Porte (Cambridge, 1982), p. 347.
■ George Washington's quotation on p. 6 is from Washington's *Writings*, ed. J. C. Fitzpatrick (Washington, 1938), xxvii, 252; xxxiv, 23. Emphasis added.
■ John Quincy Adams's quotation on p. 7 is from a letter written by Adams to Baron von Furstenwaerther and published in Werner Sollors' book *Beyond Ethnicity* (New York, 1986), p. 4. Emphasis added.
■ Alexis de Tocqueville's first quotation on p. 7 is from a letter written by Tocqueville to Ernest de Chabrol dated June 9, 1831, and published in Tocqueville's *Selected Letters on Politics and Society*, ed. Roger Boesche (Berkeley, 1985), p. 38.
■ Tocqueville's quotation on p. 7 is from his book *Democracy in America*, vol. I (1835), chap. xiv.
■ James Bryce's quotation on p. 7 is from his book *The American Commonwealth*, vol. II (London, 1888), pp. 709 & 328.
■ Gunnar Myrdal's quotation on p. 8 is from his book *An American Dilemma* (1944; 20th-anniversary edition, New York, 1962), chap. 1.
■ Herman Melville's quotation on p. 8 is from his book *Redburn*, chap. 33.
■ W. E. B. Du Bois's quotation on p. 9 is from his book *Dusk of Dawn* (Harcourt, Brace & Co., 1940). Also published in *Writings* (New American Library), p. 563.
■ Abraham Lincoln's quotation on p. 9 is from a letter written by Lincoln to Joshua F. Speed dated August 24, 1855, and published in Lincoln's *Speeches and Writings, 1832-1858* (Library of America), p. 363.
■ Frederick Jackson Turner's quotation on p. 9 is from his book *The Frontier in American History* (New York, 1920), pp. 22-23.
■ James Bryce's quotation on pp. 9-10 is from *The American Commonwealth*, vol. II, p. 329.
■ Henry James's quotations on pp. 10 & 11 are from his book *The American Scene* (1906; Horizon Press edition,

1967) pp. 64, 120-121, 132, & 139.
■ *The Melting-Pot* and Jane Addams's quotation on pp. 11 & 12 are from Arthur Mann's book *The One and the Many* (Chicago, 1979), pp. 98-100, 110, & 192; and Milton Gordon's book *Assimilation in American Life* (New York, 1964), pp. 120-121.
■ The quotation from a Jewish reviewer on p. 12 is from Arthur Mann's *The One and the Many*, p. 113.
■ Woodrow Wilson's quotation on p. 13 is from his address to foreign-born citizens on May 10, 1915, in Philadelphia, which was published in Wilson's *The Messages and Papers of Woodrow Wilson*, ed. Albert Shaw (New York, 1924), vol. I, pp. 115-116.
■ Theodore Roosevelt's quotation on p. 13 is from his address in New York on September 10, 1917, and published in his *Works* (Memorial edition), chap. XXI, p. 38; also from the April 16, 1918, editorial in the *Kansas City Star*, and from the book *Roosevelt in the Kansas City Star*, ed. Ralph Stout (Boston, 1921), p. 137.
■ Horace Kallen's quotations on pp. 13 & 14 are from the February 18 & 25, 1915, issues of *The Nation* and from his book *Culture and Democracy in the United States* (New York, 1924), pp. 116, 122, & 124.
■ Nicholas Roosevelt's quotation on p. 13 is from *The New York Times* and Arthur Mann's *The One and the Many*, p. 142.
■ Franklin D. Roosevelt's quotation on p. 14 is from a letter to Henry L. Stimson dated February 1, 1943. The occasion, ironically, was the formation of a combat team of American citizens of Japanese ancestry. The first sentence quoted was written by Elmer Davis, distinguished journalist and head of the Office of War Information; see Bill Hosokawa's *Nisei: The Quiet Americans* (New York, 1969), pp. 365-366.
■ Alexis de Tocqueville's quotation on p. 14 is from his book *Democracy in America*, vol. I, chap. xviii.
■ Gunnar Myrdal's quotation on p. 15 is from *An American Dilemma*, pp. 4, 13, 809, & 880.
■ Marcus Lee Hansen's quotation on p. 16 is from his article "The Problem of the Third Generation Immigrant," reprinted and introduced by Oscar Handlin in the November 1952 edition of *Commentary*. The second generation, according to Hansen, tended to be "traitors" who in their passion to be accepted as Americans worked overtime to divest themselves of their past—the past that the third generation, more securely American, then seeks to recover. Hansen's Law can be

pushed too far. As Werner Sollors points out, Hansen himself, Oscar Handlin (the historian who did much to popularize Hansen's Law), and my father (who long advocated the writing of immigration history and, after Hansen's premature death, put his last two books in shape for publication) were all second-generation sons of foreign-born fathers; see Sollors' *Beyond Ethnicity*, p. 218.

■ Gunnar Myrdal's quotation on p. 16 is from "The Case Against Romantic Ethnicity," Dialogue Discussion Paper, Center for the Study of Democratic Institutions, May 13, 1974, pp. 9 & 17.

■ The quotation "the unmeltable ethnics" on p. 17 is from Michael Novak's *The Rise of the Unmeltable Ethnics* (New York, 1972).

■ The passage concerning the Ethnic Heritage Studies Act on p. 17 is from Arthur Mann's *The One and the Many*, pp. 167-168.

CHAPTER 2

■ The quotation on p. 20 is from George Orwell's *1984* (New York, 1949), p. 251.

■ Ernest Gellner's quotation on p. 21 is from his book *Thought and Change* (London, 1964), p. 168.

■ J. H. Plumb's quotation on pp. 21 & 22 is from his book *The Death of the Past* (Boston, 1969), p. 40.

■ Isaiah Berlin's quotation on p. 22 is from his book *The Crooked Timber of Humanity* (London, 1990), pp. 246-247.

■ Eric Foner's quotation on p. 22 is from his article "Restructuring Yesterday's News," *Harper's*, December 1990, p. 70.

■ Saburō Ienaga's quotation on p. 23 is from his book *The Pacific War: World War II and the Japanese, 1931-1945* (New York, 1978), p. xi; see also Steven R. Weisman's article "Japan and the War: Debate on Censors is Renewed," *The New York Times*, October 8, 1989.

■ Michael Stürmer's quotation on p. 23 is from Richard J. Evans's *In Hitler's Shadow* (New York, 1989), pp. 19, 103, & 179.

■ Milan Kundera's quotation on p. 23 is from his book *The Book of Laughter and Forgetting* (1979; Penguin edition, 1981), pp. 3 & 159.

■ Vaclav Havel's quotation on p. 24 is from Henry Kamm's article "Two Heads of State Call on Waldheim," *The New York Times*, July 27, 1990.

■ The quotation from Arthur Schlesinger Jr.'s grandfather on p. 24 is from the introduction to Arthur M. Schlesinger Sr.'s *The Birth of the Nation* (New York, 1968), p. v.

■ Andrew Hacker's quotation on p. 24 is from his article "Do Schools Teach Bias to Kids?," *New York Newsday*, September 10, 1989.

■ William Hale Thompson's quotations on p. 25 are from Arthur M. Schlesinger Sr.'s book *In Retrospect: The History of a Historian* (New York, 1963), pp. 103-105.

■ John V. Kelleher's quotation on p. 25 is from his article "A Long Way From Tipperary," *Reporter*, May 12, 1960.

■ Peggy Noonan's quotation on p. 26 is from her article "What New Americans Need to Know," *The Wall Street Journal*, November 21, 1990.

■ Allan Bloom's quotation on p. 26 is from his book *The Closing of the American Mind* (New York, 1987), pp. 29 & 56.

■ Pieter Geyl's quotation on p. 26 is from his book *Napoleon For and Against* (1949; Peregrine paperback, 1965), p. 18.

■ Frederick Jackson Turner's quotation on p. 27 is from his book *The Frontier in American History*, p. 24.

■ W. E. B. Du Bois's quotation on p. 27 is from his book *Black Reconstruction* (New York, 1935), pp. 725 & 727.

■ President Kennedy's quotation on p. 27 is from Arthur M. Schlesinger Jr.'s book *A Thousand Days* (Boston, 1965), p. 966.

■ Herbert Aptheker's quotation on p. 27 is from the introduction to *William Styron's Nat Turner: Ten Black Writers Respond*, ed. John Henrik Clarke (New York, 1968), p. vii.

■ Malcolm X's quotation on p. 27 is from a leaflet advertising the Second National Conference, "The Infusion of African & African American Content in the School Curriculum," Atlanta, Georgia, November 1-4, 1990.

■ In regard to black psychologists' arguments on p. 30, see, for example, Edmund W. Gordon, Fayneese Miller, and David Rollock's article "Coping with Communicentric Bias in Knowledge Production in the Social Sciences," *Educational Researcher*, April 1990. Black scholars are no more immune than white scholars to the temptations of pretentious jargon.

■ Maulana Karenga's quotation on p. 30 is from his book *Introduction to Black Studies* (Los Angeles, 1982), pp. 42 & 43. Asante's comment is on the back cover.

■ The quotation on p. 30 from a black writer is from Larry Cuban's article "Black History and White Folk," *Saturday Review*, September 21, 1968.

■ Melville J. Herskovits' quotation on p. 30 is from his book *The Myth of the Negro Past* (New York, 1941), p. 299.

■ Jacob Gordon's quotation on p. 30 is from Isabel Wilkerson's article "Facing Grim Data on Young Males, Blacks Grope for Ways to End Blight," *The New York Times*, July 17, 1990.

■ Felix Boateng's quotation on p. 31 is from the book *Going to School: The African-American Experience*, ed. Kofi Lomotey (Albany, 1990), pp. 14, 73, & 79.

■ Maulana Karenga's quotation on p. 31 is from *Introduction to Black Studies*, pp. 25-27.

■ Molefi Kete Asante's first quotation on p. 31 is from Debra Viadero's article "Battle Over Multicultural Education Rises in Intensity," *Education Week*, November 28, 1990, p. 11. His second quotation is from Carol Innerst's article "Putting Africa on the Map," *The Washington Times*, November 13, 1990.

■ Clare Jacob's quotation on p. 31 is from Jane Caulton's article "D.C. Joins Other School Systems in Push for Afrocentric Reforms," *The Washington Times*, August 6, 1990.

■ Charles Willie's quotation on p. 31 is from Glenn M. Rickett's article "Multiculturalism Mobilizes," *Academic Questions*, summer 1990, p. 64.

■ The quotation on p. 31 attributed to a scholar is from I. A. Newby's article "Historians and Negroes," *Journal of Negro History*, January 1969, p. 33.

■ Asa Hilliard's quotation on p. 31 is from Anthony DePalma's article "The Culture Question," *The New York Times*, supplement on education, November 4, 1990.

■ Na'im Akbar's quotation on p. 32 is from Joyce Braden Harris's *African and African-American Traditions in Language Arts* (Portland Baseline Essay), p. 30.

■ Amos Wilson's quotation on p. 33 is from Maulana Karenga's *Introduction to Black Studies*, pp. 338–340.

■ Molefi Kete Asante's quotations on p. 46 are from his book *Afrocentricity* (revised edition, Trenton, 1988), pp. 1, 2, 20, 38, 43, & 67.

■ Leonard Jeffries's quotation on p. 34 is from Joseph Berger's article "Professors' Theories on Race Stir Turmoil at City College," *The New York Times*, April 20, 1990; Tim Spofford's article "State's Schools Smother Black Culture, Professor Says," *The Times Union*, Albany, New York, March 22, 1990; and Carol Innerst's article "Putting Africa on the Map."

■ The quotations about the new curriculum on pp. 34 & 35 are from "A Curriculum of Inclusion, Report of the Commissioner's Task Force on Minorities: Equity and Excellence," July 1989, pp. iii, iv, 1, 16, 21, 34, & 35, and from the appendix, pp. 9, 24, & 25. The commentator who objected to "slaves" is Cybele Raver of the Yale Department of Psychology in a memorandum to Ed Lalor of the New York State Department of Education, December 17, 1990.

■ Asa Hilliard's quotation on p. 35 is from his article "Free Your Mind, Return to the Source: The African Origin of Civilization" (mimeograph), pp. 6, 12, 19, 21, & 23.

■ John Henrik Clarke's quotation on p. 36 is from *Social Studies African-American Baseline Essay* (Portland, 1987), pp. 4, 8–11, 56, & 60.

■ The quotation on p. 36 concerning other Baseline Essays' arguments is from Michael D. Harris's book *African-American Art Traditions and Developments* (Portland, 1987), p. 2.

■ Leonard Jeffries's quotation on p. 36 is from Tim Spofford's article "State's Schools Smother Black Culture."

■ The passage concerning Napoleon on p. 36 is from Carol Innerst's article "Multiethnic Education Aims for History's Untold Stories," *The Washington Times*, November 13, 1990.

■ Edward W. Said's quotation on p. 38 is from his article "Ignorant Armies Clash by Night," *The Nation*, February 11, 1991.

CHAPTER 3

■ The quotation on p. 40 is from Roger Kimball's article "The Periphery vs. the Center: The MLA in Chicago," *The New Criterion*, February 1991, p. 17.

■ Arthur Schlesinger Jr.'s quotation on p. 41 is from his article "Nationalism and History," *Journal of Negro History*, January 1969, p. 19.

■ Frank M. Snowden Jr.'s quotation on p. 42 is from his article "Bernal's 'Blacks,' Herodotus, and Other Classical Evidence," *Arethusa*, fall 1989, pp. 83 & 84.

■ Frank J. Yurco's first quotation on p. 42 is from his article "Were the Ancient Egyptians Black or White?," *Biblical Archeology Review*, September–October 1989. His second quotation is from a letter he wrote to Erich Martel dated November 14, 1990. Mr. Martel has done yeoman work in trying to persuade the Washington school system of the sham scholarship involved in the Afrocentric curriculum.

■ Miriam Lichtheim's quotation on p. 42 is from a letter she wrote to Erich Martel dated July 25, 1990.

■ Afaf Marsot's quotation on p. 42 is from Steve Duin's article "A Return to Segregationist History," *Portland Oregonian*, November 18, 1990.

■ Carter Woodson's quotation on p. 43 is from his book *The Negro in Our History* (Washington, 1922), p. 10.

■ The passage from L. Pearce Williams on p. 43 is from his letter "Did Egypt Originate Geometry Theorem?," *The New York Times*, February 14, 1991.

■ Diane Ravitch's quotation on p. 43 is from her article "Multiculturalism," *American Scholar*, summer 1990, p. 347.

■ First quotation on p. 43 is from H. H. Adams III's essay "African and African-American Contributions to Science and Technology" (Portland, 1987), p. 77. For the correction (and a multitude of other facts and insights) I am indebted to Diane Ravitch. Rayford Logan's quotation is from *Dictionary of American Negro Biography* (New York, 1982), p. 192.

■ Bill Graves is the reporter quoted on p. 43. His quotation comes from his article "Africanized History Opens Eyes," *Portland Oregonian*, November 18, 1990.

■ Wade Nobles's quotation on p. 44 is from Maulana Karenga's *Introduction to Black Studies*.

■ Léopold Senghor's quotation on p. 44 is from Roger Shattuck and Samba Ka's article "Born Again African," *The New York Review of Books*, December 20, 1990.

■ David Walker's quotation on p. 45 is from Lawrence H. Fuchs's book *The American Kaleidoscope* (Hanover, 1990), p. 151.

■ Wilson J. Moses' quotation on p. 45 is from his article "The Abolitionist as Hero," *The Washington Post Book World*, January 20, 1991.

■ The quotation on p. 45 is from David Gerber's *Black Ohio and the Color Line, 1860-1915* (Urbana, 1976), p. 182; see also Judith Stein's quotation in *The Invention of Ethnicity*, edited by Werner Sollors (New York, 1989), p. 81.

■ W. E. B. Du Bois's quotation on p. 45 is from *Dusk of Dawn*, p. 116, and from *Writings* (Library of America), pp. 639 & 755; see also *W.E.B. Du Bois: A Reader*, ed. Meyer Weinberg (New York, 1970), p. 373; and Orlando Patterson's article "Rethinking Black History," *Harvard Educational Review*, August 1971, p. 310. Emphasis added.

■ Abram L. Harris's quotation on p. 45 is from his book *Race, Radicalism, and Reform*, and from J. S. Butler's article "Multiple Identities," *Society*, May-June 1990, p. 9.

■ Horace Mann Bond's quotation on p. 45 is from *The New York Times*, June 27, 1959; see also Milton Gordon's book *Assimilation in American Life*, pp. 15 & 113.

■ Martin Luther King Jr.'s quotation on p. 46 is from Robert Penn Warren's book *Who Speaks for the Negro?* (New York, 1965), p. 216.

■ The passage concerning Alex Haley on p. 46 is from Werner Sollors' *The Invention of Ethnicity*, p. 227.

■ LeRoi Jones's quotation on p. 46 is from his book *Home* (New York, 1966), p. 111.

■ The passage on p. 46 concerning Arthur Smith is from Molefi Kete Asante's book *Afrocentricity*, p. 29; see also William Raspberry's article "Euro, Afro and Other Eccentric 'Centrics,'" *The Washington Post*, September 10, 1990.

■ Wade Nobles's quotation on p. 47 is from accounts by Andrew Sullivan in his article "Racism 101," *The New Republic*, November 26, 1990, and by Carol Innerst in her article "Multiethnic Education Aims for History's Untold Stories," *The Washington Post*, November 13, 1990.

■ Nathan Huggins's quotation on p. 47 is from his article in *Center Magazine*, July-August 1974; see also Werner Sollors' *Beyond Ethnicity*, pp. 13 & 14.

■ The passage on p. 47 concerning Professor Asante is from his April 6, 1989, lecture at Rider College, cited in A. F. Scrupski's article "Multiculturalism: Political Wolf Under Educational Sheepskin," *Measure*, February-March 1990, p. 4.

■ William Raspberry's quotation on p. 47 is from his article "Euro, Afro and Other Eccentric 'Centrics.'"

■ The passage on p. 50 concerning *The Washington Post*-ABC poll is from the article "Men and Women of Their Word," *The Washington Post National Weekly Edition*, October 28-November 4, 1990; see also the article "Poll Says Most Blacks Prefer 'Black' to 'African-American,'" *The New York Times*, January 29, 1991.

■ Henry Adams's quotation on p. 50 is from his book *Education*, chap. xvi.

■ Asa Hilliard's quotation on p. 50 is from David Nicholson's article "'Afrocentrism' and the Tribalization of America," *The Washington Post*, September 23, 1990.

■ Frederick Douglass's quotation on p. 51 is from his book *Narrative of the Life of . . . an American Slave* (1845; Anchor paperback, 1989), pp. 42 & 43, and his book *My Bondage and My Freedom* (New York, 1855), pp. 156-158.

■ W.E.B. Du Bois's quotation on p. 51 is from his book *The Souls of Black Folk*; see also *Writings* (Library of America), p. 438.

■ Ralph Ellison's first quotation on p. 51 is from Jim Sleeper's book *The Closest of Strangers* (New York, 1990), p. 234; his later quotation was from *The New Republic*, December 24, 1990.

■ Sterling A. Brown, Arthur P. Davis, and Ulysses Lee's quotation on p. 51 are from the book they edited, *The Negro Caravan: Writings by American Negroes* (New York, 1941), pp. 6 & 7.

■ William Raspberry's quotation on p. 52 is from his article "Euro, Afro and Other Eccentric 'Centrics.'"

■ Jacques Barzun's quotation on p. 52 is from a letter from Barzun to Diane Ravitch dated February 26, 1991.

■ A. A. Schomburg's quotation on p. 53 is from Benjamin Quarles's article "What the Historian Owes the Negro," *Saturday Review*, September 3, 1966.

■ Orlando Patterson's quotation on p. 53 is from his article "Rethinking Black History," p. 305.

■ John Hope Franklin's quotation on p. 53 is from his book *Race and History* (Baton Rouge, 1989), p. ix.

■ Henry Louis Gates Jr.'s quotation on p. 53 is from *The Detroit News*, January 31, 1991.

■ Asa Hilliard's quotation on p. 53 is from Bill Graves's article "Africanized History Opens Eyes."

■ Don Smith, chairman of the education department at City University of New York's Baruch College, is the author defending the New York task-force report quoted on p. 53. He is also quoted in Katti Gray's article "Black Group Rallying for Curriculum," *Newsday*, July 22, 1990.

■ Diane Ravitch's quotations on pp. 53 & 54 are from her article "History and the Perils of Pride" (manuscript); see also Debra Viadero's articles "History Curricula Stir Controversy in Largest State," *Education Week*, August 1, 1990, and "Battle Over Multicultural Education Rises in Intensity," *Education Week*, November 28, 1990; and Dexter Waugh's article "California Minorities Fight 'Chauvinistic' School Books," *Washington Times*, January 30, 1991.

■ The passage concerning the Iroquois lobby on p. 54 is from Diane Ravitch's article "Multiculturalism," *American Scholar*, summer 1990, pp. 346 & 347; and William A. Starna's letter "Whose History Will Be Taught?," *The New York Times*, March 7, 1990.

■ Alan L. Benosky is the retired state history teacher quoted on p. 54 from his letter to *Newsday*, July 15, 1990.

■ The quotation on pp. 54 & 55 is from the Department of History at the State University of New York and a letter from Kenneth P. O'Brien, the chair of the SUNY Brockport history department, to CUNY Graduate School, dated November 25, 1990.

■ Franklyn Jenifer's quotation on p. 55 is from Jacob Weisburg's interview with Jenifer, "Franklyn Jenifer: Taking Howard University Into Slum Neighborhoods," *The Los Angeles Times*, February 10, 1991.

- Gore Vidal's quotation on p. 55 is from Jon Wiener's article "The Scholar Squirrels and the National Security State: An Interview with Gore Vidal," *Radical History Review*, spring 1989, p. 136.

CHAPTER 4

- William Raspberry's quotation on p. 58 is from his article "Euro, Afro and Other Eccentric 'Centrics.'"
- Chief Justice Warren's quotation on p. 59 is from *Brown* v. *Board of Education of Topeka*, 347 U.S. 483 (1954).
- Janice Hale-Benson's quotation on p. 59 is from *Going to School: The African-American Experience*, ed. Kofi Lomotey, pp. 82 & 216.
- Dinesh D'Souza's quotation on p. 59 is from his article "The New Segregation on Campus," *American Scholar*, winter 1991, p. 20.
- Alan Kors is the University of Pennsylvania professor quoted on p. 59. His quotation is from Mona Charen's article "A Losing Battle v. Campus Thought Police," *Newsday*, December 5, 1990.
- Jacob Weisberg's quotation on p. 59 is from his article "Thin Skins," *The New Republic*, February 18, 1991.
- The quotation on p. 60 from a black student at Central Michigan University is from the *Chronicle of Higher Education*, quoted in Dinesh D'Souza's article "The New Segregation on Campus," p. 19.
- Signithia Fordham's quotation on p. 60 is from Seth Mydans's article "Black Identity vs. Success and Seeming 'White,'" *The New York Times*, April 25, 1990.
- The quotation concerning the University of California at Berkeley's Budget Committee on p. 60 is from Stephen R. Barnett's article "Get Back," *The New Republic*, February 18, 1991.
- Henry Louis Gates's quotation on p. 60 is from *The Detroit News*, January 31, 1991.
- John Hope Franklin's quotation on p. 60 is from his book *Race and History*, p. 301.
- August Wilson's quotation on p. 60 is from his article "'I Want a Black Director,'" *The New York Times*, September 26, 1990.
- The quotation concerning Jonathan Pryce on p. 60 is from Mervyn Rothstein's article "Union Bars White in Asian Role," *The New York Times*, August 8, 1990; Joseph C. Koenenn's article "Efforts at Casting Compromise," *Newsday*, August 10, 1990. Actors' Equity later rescinded the ban against Pryce.
- Kenneth B. Clark's quotation on p. 61 is from his "Letter of Resignation From Board of Directors of Antioch College," *Black Studies: Myths & Realities*, introduced by Bayard Rustin (New York, 1969), p. 32.
- In regard to the passage about printing federal laws in German on p. 61, see the clarifying letter by Dennis Baron in the *Times Literary Supplement*, September 1-7, 1989.
- Alfredo Mathew Jr.'s quotation on p. 61 is from Rosalie Pedalino Porter's book *Forked Tongue* (New York, 1990), p. 7.

- Richard Rodriguez's first quotation on p. 62 is from his article "Unilingual, Not Unilateral," *The Wall Street Journal*, June 25, 1985. His second quotation is from his book *Hunger of Memory* (Boston, 1982), pp. 19 & 27.
- Mario Cuomo's quotation on p. 62 is from William E. Leuchtenburg's article "Most Americans Don't Know What Lincoln Really Represents," *American Heritage*, December 1990, pp. 59 & 60.
- Rosalie Pedalino Porter's quotation on p. 62 is from her book *Forked Tongue*, pp. 217 & 218. See also two other articles: "Bilingual Education Has Muted the Future for Minority Children," *Washington Post National Weekly*, April 30–May 6, 1990, and "The Case for English Immersion," *Teacher Magazine*, August 1990.
- Harold Isaacs' quotation on p. 62 is from his article "The One and the Many," *American Educator*, spring 1978, p. 9; see also Isaacs' book *Idols of the Tribe* (New York, 1975), pp. 216–218.
- William Raspberry's quotation on p. 63 is from Jason DeParle's article "Talk of Government Being Out to Get Blacks Falls on More Attentive Ears," *The New York Times*, October 29, 1990.
- Richard Rodriguez's quotation on p. 63 is from his article "Unilingual, Not Unilateral."
- The passage on p. 64 concerning posters at the University of Michigan is from Dinesh D'Souza's article "Illiberal Education," *The Atlantic*, March 1991, p. 52.
- Justice Oliver Wendell Holmes's quotation on p. 64 is from *United States* v. *Schwimmer*, 279 U.S. 644 (1928).
- For more information about the debate over the First Amendment on p. 64, see the interesting, though (for me) ultimately unconvincing, argument in Mary Ellen Gale's article "On Curbing Racial Speech," *The Responsive Community*, winter 1990-91, pp. 47-61.
- The passage concerning the American Civil Liberties Union on p. 64 is from Anthony DePalma's article "Battling Bias, Campuses Face Free Speech Fight," *The New York Times*, February 20, 1991.
- Kenneth B. Clark's quotation on p. 65 is from his "Letter of Resignation," p. 33.
- Dinesh D'Souza's comment on p. 65 is from his article "The New Segregation," p. 21.
- The bulletin from the Office of Student Affairs at Smith College on p. 65 is from John Taylor's article "Are You Politically Correct?," *New York*, January 21, 1991.
- The philosopher's quotation on p. 65 is from Mona Charen's article "A Losing Battle."
- The quotations concerning Bernard Bailyn and Stephan Thernstrom on pp. 65 & 66 are from a letter from Paula Ford and Penelope Codrington to Stephan Thernstrom dated March 9, 1988.
- Catharine Stimpson's quotation on p. 66 is from John Taylor's article "Are You Politically Correct?," p. 35.
- The quotations on p. 66 concerning correspondence between a University of Pennsylvania student and an administrator are from A. C. Kors's article "It's

Speech, Not Sex, the Dean Bans Now," *The Wall Street Journal*, October 12, 1989.

■ Theodore Roosevelt's quotation on p. 67 is from his *Works* (Memorial edition, New York, 1923–26) chap. XX, p. 456.

CHAPTER 5

■ Stephan Thernstrom's quotation on p. 71 is from his article "The Minority Majority Will Never Come," *The Wall Street Journal*, July 26, 1990.

■ For a historian's cogent discussion about the last paragraph, p. 71, see Otis Graham Jr.'s article "Immigration and the National Interest" in *U.S. Immigration in the 1980s: Reappraisal and Reform*, ed. David Simcox (Westview Press, 1988), pp. 124–136.

■ The quotation on p. 71 is from Nathan Newman to the editors of *Dissent*, summer 1989, p. 413.

■ The quotation on p. 72 concerning European classical music is from Clyde Moneyhun's letter "Culture Schlock," *The New Republic*, March 4, 1991; see also Edward Rothstein's article "Roll Over Beethoven," *The New Republic*, February 4, 1991.

■ The passage attributed to the National Endowment for the Humanities on p. 72 is from Lynne V. Cheney's book *Fifty Hours: A Core Curriculum for College Students* (Washington, 1989), p. 7.

■ The passage on p. 72 concerning required courses in third-world or ethnic studies is from Dinesh D'Souza's "Illiberal Education," p. 53.

■ Pearce Williams's quotation on p. 72 is from his article "Did Egypt Originate Geometry Theorem?"

■ Henry A. Giroux is the first professor quoted on p. 73. His quotation is from John Searle's article "The Storm Over the University," *The New York Review of Books*, December 6, 1990.

■ Stanley Hauerwas of the Duke Divinity School is the second professor quoted on p. 73. His quotation is from Pam Kelley's article "For Duke Profs, The Hot Debate Is What to Teach," *The Charlotte Observer*, September 28, 1990. I have supplied the full word that the *Observer* primly rendered as "—holes."

■ The passage about Marxists on p. 73 is from Irving

Howe's admirable essay "The Value of the Canon," *The New Republic*, February 18, 1991.

■ For more information about the collectivist cultures on p. 76, see the research described by Daniel Goleman, "The Group and the Self: New Focus on a Cultural Rift," *The New York Times*, December 25, 1990.

■ The passage on p. 77 concerning Algerian women is from Frantz Fanon's book *A Dying Colonialism* (London, 1965), pp. 37 & 46.

■ Margaret Thatcher's quotation on p. 78 is from David S. Broder's article "Her View of the U.S. Had a Euro-Cynical Bent," *International Herald Tribune*, March 13, 1991.

■ Lawrence Fuchs's quotation on p. 79 is from *The American Kaleidoscope*, p. 492.

■ Stephen Steinberg's quotation on p. 79 is from his book *The Ethnic Myth*, p. 257.

■ Richard Alba's quotation on p. 79 is from his book *Ethnic Identity: The Transformation of White America*. See the discussion in Andrew Hacker's article "Trans-National America," *The New York Review of Books*, November 22, 1990.

■ The passages on pp. 79 & 80 concerning Hispanic-Americans and historical leaders are from Lawrence Fuchs's *The American Kaleidoscope*.

■ The statistics concerning Asian-American marriages on p. 80 are from Stephan Thernstrom's article "Is America's Ethnic Revival a Fad Like Jogging?" *U.S. News & World Report*, November 17, 1980.

■ The statistics from the Census Bureau on p. 80 are from Gregory Stephens's letter "Interracial Marriage," *San Francisco Chronicle*, December 24, 1990.

■ Herbert Croly's quotations on p. 80 are from his book *The Promise of American Life* (New York, 1909), pp. 139 & 194. Croly was talking about class, not ethnic, divisions—indeed, he rather believed in the inferiority of blacks—but his general point remains sound.

■ Diane Ravitch's quotation on p. 81 is from her article "Multiculturalism," p. 339.

Additional Copies

To order additional copies of *The Disuniting of America* for friends or colleagues, please write to The Larger Agenda Series, Whittle Books, 505 Market St., Knoxville, Tenn. 37902. For a single copy, please enclose a check for $11.95 payable to The Larger Agenda Series. When ordering 10 or more books, enclose $9.95 for each; for orders of 50 or more, enclose $7.95 for each. If you wish to order by phone, call 800-284-1956.

Also available, at the same prices, are copies of the previous books in The Larger Agenda Series: *The Trouble With Money* by William Greider, *Adhocracy: The Power to Change* by Robert H. Waterman Jr., *Life After Television* by George Gilder, *The Book Wars* by James Atlas, *The X Factor* by George Plimpton, *A Short History of Financial Euphoria* by John Kenneth Galbraith, *Pacific Rift* by Michael Lewis, and *Predicting Russia's Future* by Richard Lourie.

Please allow two weeks for delivery.
Tennessee residents must add 7¾ percent sales tax.